THE ART OF
RAILROAD
PHOTOGRAPHY

Amtrak No. 6, the eastbound California Zephyr, emerges from one of the twin tunnel bores near Kyune, Utah, on its April Fools Day descent of Soldier Summit. Canon T90, 50 mm, Fujichrome 50, 1/250th, f5.6

THE ART OF
RAILROAD
PHOTOGRAPHY

Techniques for taking dynamic trackside pictures

GARY J. BENSON

A special thanks to **Canon**, who in part made this book possible

This book is dedicated to all photographers, past and present, who have shared the passion and excitement of making great train images.

Several people were instrumental in helping me put together this book. Special thanks go to Paul Brooks, Fred Frailey, Phil Maggitti, and Billy Prouty for the time they took to edit and proofread either the entire text or portions thereof. I'd also like to thank Mike Del Vecchio and Bruce Kelly at *Railfan and Railroad Magazine* and Bob Shell at *Shutterbug* for the technical data they provided. Many thanks to Kevin Keefe at *Trains* for his belief in this book when it was only the seed of an idea, his foreword, and, in conjunction with Dave Ingles, his editorial instincts to use my photos in their magazine. Lastly, but most especially, I'd like to thank my wife and business partner Susan for her hours of patience when we are trackside, as well as her enormous editing and word processing efforts. Thanks!

Canon logo is trademarked. Used with permission

To order additional copies of this book or other Kalmbach books, call toll free at (800) 533-6644

Library of Congress Cataloging-in-Publication Data

Benson, Gary J.
    The art of railroad photography : techniques for taking dynamic
  trackside pictures / Gary J. Benson.
      p. cm.
    Includes index.
    ISBN 0-89024-133-3
    1. Photography of railroads. 2. Railroads--United States-
-Pictorial works. I. Title.
TR715.B45 1993
  778.9'6252--dc20   93-4734

Contents

A light snow has dusted the mountain tops along Union Pacific's Caliente Subdivision several miles south of Caliente, Nevada. Engine 3269 and three other SD40-2s are powering their eastbound tonnage over a historic route, originally known as the San Pedro, Los Angeles & Salt Lake Railroad.
Canon F-1, 200 mm, Fujichrome 100, 1/250th, f4.5

Foreword

This is a book I wish I had in 1966 when, as a Michigan teenager, I first pointed my parents' clumsy Argus C3 camera down the New York Central mainline and brought the onrushing Chicago-bound Wolverine into focus. I didn't know what I was doing, but a year of reading TRAINS Magazine had convinced me that taking "train pictures" was a hobby worth pursuing. I remember the slightly scary sight of train 17's E7 diesel looming in the viewfinder, bearing down on me at 79 mph as the shutter clicked.

In that microsecond was born a lifelong hobby. The photo turned out poorly (alas, I neglected to save it), but the experience proved irresistible, and I've been back to trackside thousands of times since. I'd like to think that over the years I've improved as a photographer; once in awhile my slides are even decent. But there is always more to learn, and that's where this book by Gary J. Benson comes in.

It would be hard to think of someone better qualified to write such a book. As a professional lensman, Gary has built an unassailable background over the past 16 years. His breakthrough book, "Rolling Thunder," won praise from quarters as diverse as railfan newsletters and The New York Times. Critic Lou Jacobs Jr., writing for the American Society of Magazine Photographers, compared Gary to Walker Evans, the influential Depression-era photojournalist.

Fortunately for us, Gary has an affinity for railroading. The technical quality of his photos is obvious. He clearly is in complete command of all the elements of photography. But Gary's images are more than the products of a skilled technician. In nearly every frame, Gary manages to milk the emotion and mystery from railroading.

I remember the day Gary and the *Trains* staff discovered each other. It was in the summer of 1988, as we made plans for our new photo magazine, *Trains Illustrated*, the debut issue of which featured six pages of Gary's work. You must realize, we see thousands of photos in the mail each month. They run the gamut from poor 5x7 drugstore prints to entire portfolios of excellent transparencies, from roster photos to all-out action. Despite this mass of material, Gary's slides jumped out at us when we opened the mysterious envelope from Bernardsville, NJ. The trademarks of a Gary Benson railroad photo were immediately apparent: a translucent, almost ethereal quality of light; imaginative placement of the train in its environment (generously, he gives the train some track over which to roll); and the elusive human element, present in his masterful portraits of railroaders at work.

Gary joins a long line of great rail photographers. I've argued with non-railroad enthusiasts and other skeptics about the merits of shooting trains and I'm sticking by my guns: Railroad photography is a discipline in its own right. It's a school of art and journalism as worthy of recognition as the fields of landscape, sports, or fashion photography, and it has its own traditions and heroes. Consider the early 20th-century images by such pioneers as Fred Jukes and Alfred W. Johnson; or the action shots of the thirties and forties by Lucius Beebe or R.H. Kindig; or the postwar innovations of Philip R. Hastings, Richard Steinheimer, Don Wood, and Richard J. Cook; or the daring work of today's young lions. There is a continuum here, a tradition we can respect, even cherish. It is also something Gary plugs into every time he and his wife and business partner, Susan Benson, head out on another of their cross-country railroad forays.

All that said, railroad photography is not some sort of precious or exclusive art form open only to a select few. If anything, it is an egalitarian hobby. Whether you're a weekend train-chaser or seasoned pro the essential elements of the experience always are the same—you need a camera, film, light, a train, and some luck. You don't have to buy tickets, or hire models, or trot around the globe. Find a busy mainline, crank up your scanner, and wait for the big show. Railroading's appeal will speak for itself. And the rewards can be rich.

Railroad photography has been crying out for a book like this for decades. We can be grateful that Gary Benson has given it to us.

Kevin P. Keefe
Editor
TRAINS Magazine
Waukesha, Wisconsin
September 1993

On August 12, 1992, two General Electric C40-8W's ease Conrail unit coal train UAN-10 down from Bailey mine on the Monongahela Railway's Manor Branch near Time, Pennsylvania. The MGA, owned and operated by Conrail, is a small but busy coal-hauling road based in extreme southwestern Pennsylvania. Canon EOS-1, 80-200-mm zoom set at 200 mm, Fuji Velvia 50, 1/500th, f4.5

Exercising running rights on Conrail's Souther Tier Line at Canaseraga, New York, four Susquehanna locomotives cruise along with a Sea-Land stack train in tow. Canon F-1, 300 mm, Fujichrome 100, 1/500th, f4

Preface

Capturing the drama of trains and railroading has been a challenge to photographers for more than a century. My own challenge began in 1986 with two exploratory trips in the western states to photograph trains of the Union Pacific, Santa Fe, and Southern Pacific. From a purely aesthetic standpoint I was successful and made many nice images. Yet, I felt something was missing. I wasn't seeing the whole picture. I needed information on railroads and, more specifically, on photographing trains rumbling down tracks. My search for a book or magazine that would introduce me to the hobby of railfanning went on fruitlessly for months. Bits of information trickled my way via Trains magazine and a series of books by the late Don Ball Jr., but much of it was too advanced for me to comprehend then. Only through research along with trial and error did I find satisfaction in railroad photography and an understanding of railroad operations.

I decided to write this book while the frustration at the lack of material on railroad photography was still fresh in my mind. In the following pages I share what I've learned about producing interesting and dynamic train pictures. But first a warning: This is not an exhaustive study of railroad photography. Instead, it is an overview that reflects my tastes and my preferences — in camera equipment, film, subjects, and so on. Thus, I avoid lengthy camera and film comparisons and concentrate on the techniques I use — and that you can adopt no matter what the equipment — to produce interesting prints and slides.

To take full advantage of this book, however, you should know the basics of photography. Finding good sources to teach you the fundamentals is not difficult. Books and magazines on photography are plentiful, as are classes that cater to just about every schedule and experience level. You could also join a camera club. Whatever path you choose, you'll be glad you spent the time and effort.

Of course, nothing rivals the experience of getting out there and taking photo after photo of just about anything: cars, football games, sunrises, sunsets, and, yes, trains. The experience you gain composing, focusing, and exposing roll after roll of film will help you months and years later when you instinctively pick up your camera, point, shoot, and capture that one special moment along the rails.

Other Things to Remember

• Photography involves compromise. Often, the compromise is money versus quality or money versus convenience. For example, you either have to pay more money to get a faster lens or you may need to shoot with more expensive, higher speed film, which produces grainier pictures. Be aware that as you select and use cameras, lenses, filters, films, and labs, you will be challenged regularly, and your image quality will be compromised in one way or another. Like it or not photography is an expensive hobby. Cheap components rarely, if ever, benefit the user. However, don't get caught up in the "I need an arsenal of expensive photo equipment to make great train photos!" trap. Sophisticated cameras and lenses are only tools to assist you in creating exciting images. After all, a writer isn't accomplished just because he or she uses a high-priced computer with a high-powered thesaurus.

• Good photography isn't about how much film you shoot per day or how many yellow or green boxes are gathering dust in your closet. Good photography is about well-composed, properly focused, and exposed images that command attention and bring pleasure to the viewer. And that includes yourself.

• Patience is valuable in railroad photography. Don't feel pressured to take your best railroad pictures in one day, one weekend, or even one year. Instead, try to get a handful of nice shots or maybe one great shot each day you are trackside. Over a period of time, your efforts will pay off in the form of a sizeable library of top-notch images.

• Be discriminating. Except when you are starting out, it's rarely worthwhile to shoot every single train you encounter. Be selective and wait until the conditions are right: a good-looking train, an interesting location, nice light. It's okay to let trains roll by while you watch and study them. Sometimes, cameras can insulate or separate you from truly experiencing the moment. But always be prepared to shoot, just in case you happen upon a unique locomotive or "foreign" power on a detouring train.

• Above all, be careful when you are trackside. Trains can appear suddenly, causing surprise and perhaps injury. No photograph is worth losing life or limb.

Whether you chase trains across county or country, keep these thoughts in mind. Good luck, and good shooting!

Gary J. Benson
Bernardsville, New Jersey
September 1993

Cameras, lenses, and accessories

The advent of the 35 millimeter single lens reflex (SLR) camera in the late 1940s heralded a new era for railroad photographers. Fortunately, the compact and versatile SLR has experienced a remarkable and continuous transformation in the last 45 years, growing smaller, lighter, and more sophisticated with each new model.

Premiere photo equipment manufacturers such as Canon, Minolta, Nikon, and Olympus offer cameras that fall into the following basic categories: mechanical, electronic, and electronic/autofocus. The brand and type you choose depends on your personal taste, experience, anticipated needs and finances. Many new camera purchases today can approach and even surpass the $1,000 level. But with reasonable care and occasional maintenance you can expect to get easily ten, twelve, or fifteen years of service from your equipment.

My Choice of Cameras

I use the Canon F-1, T90, and EOS 1 cameras to create images of railroad scenes. Although I prefer Canon, other manufacturers, such as Nikon, Minolta, and Olympus, offer cameras of high quality. Use the following comments about the F-1, T90, and EOS-1 as guideposts to assist you in selecting the camera that's best for you.

I use the F-1 (used manually with match-needle metering) because its rugged and functions well in adverse conditions, from extreme cold to soaking wet. With the motor drive attached to the F-1, the considerable weight provides me with extra stability when I'm working with a long telephoto lens or a slow shutter speed.

The Canon T90 (electronic) includes what every new 35-mm camera should:

• A small, built-in 4.5-frame-per-second motor drive with autofilm/loading autofilm rewind that allows you to shoot faster and to change rolls of film more quickly.

• An automatic film-speed sensor, which sets the film's ISO when used with DX-coded film cassettes.

• Multiple shooting modes, including manual, aperture priority, and shutter priority, plus numerous program modes.

• Three switchable metering patterns — average, partial, and spot — for versatile and accurate light readings.

• 1/250th of a second flash synchronization for greater flash/ambient light exposure control.

• 1/2-step shutter speeds (such as 1/350th, 1/750th, and so on) for increased exposure control.

The EOS-1 is the flagship of the Canon fleet and contains the latest in electronic autofocus technology. The most notable of its advances (beyond those already integrated from the T90) include:

• Autoexposure bracketing that instantaneously varies the exposure, over and under, of every 2d and 3d frame of film in three-shot sequences. This feature is exceptionally valuable in difficult or backlit situations.

• A unique quick control dial on the camera back that affords complete exposure control (aperture and shutter speed) with just one hand.

• Eight custom function controls that allow you to tailor specific aspects of the camera to your own requirements.

• A full line of excellent autofocus lenses.

• An optional power motor drive booster that increases the built-in motor drive speed from 2.5 to 5.5 frames per second and improves autofocus performance.

• Several dedicated flash units for total exposure automation and control.

Even the finest glass in many supertelephoto lenses can't cut through the radiant heat emitting from the rails, concrete ties, and ballast of some midday summer scenes. The only alternative is to shoot in the cooler hours of morning, when the sun's rays have yet to bake into the roadbed, or during the cooler fall, winter, and spring months.

This image of a westbound Amtrak Metroliner was made at Deans, New Jersey, on the Northeast Corridor. Though technically flawed by the mirage, it's an aesthetically acceptable photograph.

Canon F-1, 800-mm, Fujichrome 100, 1/500th, f 6.7

Supertelephoto lenses 400 mm, 500 mm, 600 mm, and 800 mm create these train-looks-as-though-it's-right-on-top-of-you shots while allowing the photographer to maintain a safe distance along the right of way.

Near Higgins, Texas, on the Pan Handle subdivision, Santa Fe No. 981 rounds a curve at 6:45p.m. on April 22, 1989. Canon F-1, 400 mm, Fujichrome 100, 1/500th, f5.6

Most other manufacturers offer cameras with similar features; check with your camera shop.

The Advantages of an Extra Camera Body

I work with three cameras because of the tremendous flexibility they provide in capturing a certain scene or situation. Plus, I'm able to make several images of the same train from different perspectives while it is coming down the tracks since I generally use a variety of focal length lenses simultaneously. (More about lenses later.) Of course, it's not necessary to use three, or even two, cameras to make great railroad photographs. A single SLR with a few choice lenses is adequate for most situations you'll encounter. However, an extra camera body sure helps. It provides the capability to shoot with varied film stocks or different lenses as well as act as a backup if your primary camera happens to malfunction or is damaged. Don't hesitate to consider a used body as a backup. Many fine preowned or early model cameras are available at reasonable prices.

Mechanical versus Electronic

Often I'm asked if I prefer mechanical or electronic types. Generally, I recommend the electronic type because of the advanced metering systems, built-in motor drives, and overall reduced size and weight considerations. Yet, I confess that most of the time I use my completely autoexposure-capable cameras in the manual-exposure mode. This way, I control the shutter speed and aperture. It's a steady concern that the camera's light meter will be fooled by the intense brightness of a locomotive's headlight or an occasional reflection. If I need to shoot on automatic, I use the shutter priority mode. In this mode, you select shutter speed, which remains constant as the aperture changes according to the subject's reflectance.

The only significant drawback of an entirely electronic model is the camera's total dependence on batteries. Simply put: no power, no pictures. This is important especially with many current model cameras that are dependent on the somewhat hard to find 6-volt lithium batteries. So keep plenty of spares on hand, and keep your camera protected during cold weather use. During extended winter shooting, I purchase small, inexpensive chemical-type hand warmers (available at sporting goods stores) and secure them with rubber bands to all my cameras next to the battery packs.

Motor Drives and Film Winders

Motor drives and film winders are essential. You can rely on them to help produce numerous useable images of the same train or other railroad subjects. All three of my 35-mm cameras are motor driven. I prefer to shoot a few extra frames of slide film — called in-camera duping — at 45¢ per frame than to pay $1.00 or more per dupe. Besides, I've found no lab capable of making dupes that are close to the quality of my originals.

There is another important reason that I count on motor drives. They allow me to concentrate 100

Virtually all lens manufacturers make lens shades designed to fit their line of lenses. Several aftermarket accessory companies produce them as well. Use lens shades on all your optics, all the time, even for night shots. They not only eliminate flare from the sun's rays and errant reflections, but the rigid type also offer significant protection to your lens if you drop it. Additionally, in rain or snow they keep moisture off of the front element of your lens.

Southern Pacific No. 8364 is one of 234 SD40T-2 Tunnel motors built by EMD for the railroad between 1974 and 1980. This one smokes its way up the Tehachapi mountains in California with three other EMD units on an eastbound freight. The train has already traversed over 42 miles of torturous, sustained ascent, but the 2.3 percent grade here at milepost 355 on the Mojave Subdivision will soon ease. The mountain summit, just east of the town of Tehachapi, is only seven miles away. Canon F-1, 200 mm, Fujichrome 100, 1/500th, f5.6, lens shade supplemented by a rolled-up road atlas

percent of my attention on composing and following the action of a fast freight snaking its way through an S curve — an advantage not available when your film is manually advanced. I would advise against purchasing a motor drive or winder for a camera if you shoot primarily black-and-white or color negative film and can get reprints made of choice frames or if you own only one or two lenses. Then your first priority should be to buy supplementary lenses.

Autofocus Cameras

The growth and refinement of autofocus technology over the last few years presents photographers with several entirely new camera/lens systems from which to choose. Although it would be inappropriate here to review this gear in depth, several of the more popular offerings are worthy of mention. The top of the line Canon EOS-1, the A2E, and the midpriced EOS-10S and Elan, accompanied by the EF arsenal of lenses, produce unsurpassed photographic images. The Minolta Maxxum cameras — 9000, 8000i and 9xi — with their AF lenses are capable of also producing outstanding results. Additionally, Nikon's F-4, N90, N6006, and N8008S cameras with their AF/AI-s lenses yield excellent photos as well. **5**

At first glance, all this autofocus equipment might appear to be practical for limited use by only a few sports, newspaper, or nature photographers. But autofocus benefits all shooters, even those of us who photograph trains. Those benefits include the ability to ensure razor-sharp focus when shooting in low or trying light conditions (including twilight), when using telephoto lenses wide open (and the subsequent shallow depth of field is a problem), and when you wear glasses or suffer vision impairment.

The most significant benefit you get from autofocus equipment, however, is the ability to bring instantly into focus almost any subject appearing in the AF frame of the viewfinder and to tirelessly follow this focus as the subject moves back and forth, left to right, or up and down. This advantage becomes apparent when you use an autofocus camera around a railyard where you are presented with many fleeting opportunities to make interesting images of people, equipment, and details: train crews boarding, travelers moving about, and locomotives shuttling around. With a camera such as the Canon EOS-10S and a long lens, you can compose and shoot, working quickly and instinctively. The same holds true when you are shooting trains coming down the main line.

Also, bear in mind two other thoughts about autofocus. First, you can deactivate the AF mode and focus manually while still getting the benefit of all the other hi-tech wizardry. Secondly, many of the earlier manual cameras are obsolete. No more will be made, and the supply will soon dry up.

Lenses for 35-mm Cameras

One of the most important and attractive aspects of using 35-mm equipment is the capability to change lenses quickly, alowing you to create different moods and to alter the impact of your photographs.

Ultrawide-angle lenses, with their broad field of view, allow you to include a great amount of information in a railroad scene, be it a trainscape, a locomotive cab, or an interlocking tower interior.

(Above) At Hyndman, Pennsylvania, CSX operator Pete Kelly tends to some paperwork during his late afternoon shift at Q Tower. The Armstrong interlocking levers stand ready for the evening rush of traffic. Canon F-1, 20 mm, Fujichrome 100, 1/15th, f4, tripod

(Below) For a little over an hour now these three SD40-2s, accompanied by a fuel tender, have been shoving on the rear of a BN 15,000 ton unit coal train on Nebraska's Crawford Hill, a 1.55 percent grade. Passing through a huge earthen cut near Belmont, the helpers will be cut off in another few minutes and will return to their base at Crawford for the next assignment. Canon T90, 24 mm, Fujichrome 50, 1/250th, f6.7

Telephoto lenses in the 200-mm to 400-mm range compress the elements of a scene. This creates layers of color and contrast that add a three-dimensional quality to a photograph.

Such was the case in mid-1989, as an ex-Reading Railroad GP39-2 set out cars in the decrepit remains of Delaware and Hudson's Oneonta, New York, yard. Canon T90, 300mm, Fujichrome 50, 1/250th f4

A second camera body opens up an entirely new dimension to a railroad photographer. First, it enables you to photograph the same subject from the same perspective with different lenses. This provides multiple shots of the same train which are significantly different from each other. Second, you can use a second film stock to achieve other effects and purposes.

Near Rawlings, Maryland, CSX No. R316, an eastbound mixed freight, rumbles along on the Mountain subdivision on a hot, humid June day behind seven 4-axle **locomotives.** Vertical — Canon T90, 50 mm, Fujichrome 50, 1/250th, f4; Horizontal — Canon F-1, 200 mm, Fujichrome 100, 1/250th, f5.6

Lenses are classified by focal length. Essentially they fall into six groups: ultrawide angle, wide angle, standard, telephoto, super telephoto, and zoom. All of these can be used effectively in a variety of railroad settings.

Ultrawide-angle lenses have the widest angle of view and especially are useful for photographing the cramped interiors of towers or locomotive cabs. Used outdoors, they can help produce dramatic trainscapes — my version of a train shot combined with a beautiful landscape. Besides allowing lots of information to be included in a shot, these lenses can be used to create a spatial separation between the foreground, subject, and background. However, avoid distorting your subject's appearance by shooting at an oblique angle. Common-length lenses in this group include 14 mm, 17 mm, 20 mm and 24 mm.

Wide-angle lenses are routinely more practical to use than ultrawide angles because the wide angle has less severe distortion. Either 28-mm or 35-mm lenses should be included with your other lens selections. Both are effective choices for locomotive "roster" shots and are useful for all-around shooting, including photographing groups of people.

Lenses of 45 mm, 50 mm and 55 mm are considered standard lenses because they show subjects in a scene in roughly the same size as they are viewed by human eyes. Standard lenses are often purchased with a camera as an outfit and therefore are among the most popular lens owned. They are good choices for general train photography because of their large maximum apertures of f1.8, 1.4, and 1.2, which make them especially useful in low light.

Telephoto lenses range from 85 mm to 300 mm, with common focal lengths in between at 100 mm, 135 mm, and 200 mm. Telephotos narrow the angle of view and bring distant subjects closer, which eliminates distracting background features. The 85-mm, 100-mm and 135-mm lenses are traditionally excellent choices for making portraits and are effective when photographing railroad workers.

Super telephoto lenses include the 400 mm, 500 mm, 600 mm and 800 mm. Under the right conditions — that is, cool, clear, bright, sunny days — they can be used to create dynamic "this-train-looks-like-it's-right-on-top-of-you!!!" shots without the fear of being too close. Long lenses like these compress the elements of a scene while they simultaneously create layers of depth to make a more interesting photo.

Zoom lenses (also called variable-focal-length lenses) incorporate elements inside the lens that move in relationship to the other elements, thus offering a variety of different focal lengths. Numerous versions are available, but some of the more typical lens lengths range from 28-70 mm, 35-105 mm, 70-210 mm, and 100-200 mm. Zooms are ideal for when the overall weight of your outfit is a serious concern and you routinely hike to remote locations.

There are other lens groups, such as macro, fisheye, and perspective control. But the six main groups I've outlined are the most practical for railroad photography.

Three significant factors relating to cost, value, and image quality come into play when it comes to lens selection: lens manufacturer, lens type (fixed-focal length lens or zoom), and maximum aperture (largest lens opening).

Camera Manufacturers' Lenses vs. After Market Lenses

Lenses are the single most vital link in the photographic chain. We need accurate, fine-grained film and precise, durable cameras as well. However, what good would all of our endeavors, precious time, and (often great) expense amount to if we made image after image with inferior optics?

Understand that years ago titans like Canon and Nikon established their reputations by designing, manufacturing, and selling the finest lenses available. That proud tradition continues today. That's why I am amazed to see so many advanced amateur photographers using two, sometimes three first-rate Canon or Nikon cameras sporting after-market lenses.

Expecting great performance from a Canon F-1 outfitted with a generic brand lens is like expecting great performance from your Porsche 911 with a rebuilt 40-horsepower Volkswagen engine installed. Sure the car starts and stops. It may even run at 60 miles per hour. But it doesn't provide you with the optimum performance you anticipated.

The difference between a good lens and a bad lens lies in the quality of the glass and the assembly of the optics. These two factors determine the overall sharpness, clarity, contrast, and color rendition of your photographs.

That's not to say that quality after-market lenses don't exist. They do. However, it's not easy to sort through the dozens, even hundreds, of offerings available and come up with a lens or two that may equal those offered by Canon, Minolta, Nikon, and Olympus. Even more rare is the generic lens that will surpass the quality of camera manufacturers' optics.

My own lens selection is and always has been exclusively Canon. I've used lenses made by Sigma, Tokina, and Vivitar. But I was not impressed enough by the results to switch to their equipment. (The one independent manufacturer of both manual and autofocus after-market lenses that I respect and recommend is Angenieux, although the cost of their lenses exceeds those of Canon and Nikon.)

There are only a handful of photographic filters I suggest you use for shooting trains—UV or skylight, polarizer, graduated neutral density, and graduated color. Whenever possible, however, use no filters at all. This will keep flare and image degradation to a minimum.

To darken the sky and reduce glare, I employed a polarizer to make this photo of westbound Santa Fe No. 408 threading through the semaphores just east of Wagon Mound, New Mexico. Behind the five-unit lash-up, today's "soup" (the local jargon for a train's consist) is 4,800 feet long and includes 64 loads of mixed freight and one empty. Canon T90, 35 mm, Fujichrome 50, 1/250th, f4.5

Even the most sophisticated metering systems can be fooled in difficult lighting situations. These include snow scenes, dark engines against a dark stand of trees, large shadow areas, glaring headlights, and shiny paint schemes. Therefore, use extremely high-tech auto-everything cameras in the manual exposure mode to avoid over- or under-exposing your film. Additionally, make your light readings off an area that reflects a medium percentage of light. This target can be a portion of ballast, a rock cut, weathered wood on a railroad structure, or even a dirt road. Just take your light reading a few moments prior to the train's arrival, then recompose, focus, and make your shot.

(Opposite top) In Ashland, Virginia, I metered from the ballast and a lawn to make this image of Richmond, Fredericksburg, and Potomac's Orange Blossom Special running south through the center of town in 1989. Canon F-1, 300 mm, Fujichrome 100, 1/250th, f3.5

(Opposite bottom) A late winter snowfall was sticking to everything, including eastbound Santa Fe No. 774 at Cosnino, Arizona, on February 28, 1991. The vertical faces of the rock cut to the left and right remained clear and provided a clean area to meter from. Canon F-1, 200 mm, Fujichrome 100, 1/250th, f3.5

(Above) For this commuter train east on the Raritan Valley Line at Bound Brook, I metered off some brush and overgrowth along the right of way. Canon T90, 300 mm, Fujichrome 50, 1/250th, f5.6

13

Fixed-Focal Length Lenses versus Zoom Lenses

Another important consideration affecting your choice of lenses is whether to use either fixed-focal-length or zoom lenses. As mentioned, zoom lenses have the advantage of functioning like multiple individual lenses in an all-in-one package. They save you the time spent changing lenses, and they may save you the expense of purchasing several lenses as well. I'll admit that I am a bit old fashioned when it comes to zooms (I only bought one recently), but they have two inherent disadvantages. First, I do not feel that the image quality — the sharpness, clarity, contrast and color rendition — of variable-focal-length lenses can match the outstanding results I get from my fixed-focal-length lenses. Secondly, none of the more commonly available, and relatively inexpensive, zoom lenses can come close to meeting the large maximum apertures routinely found on fixed focal-length lenses. For example, the Canon 75-200 f4.5-mm manual-focus zoom lens has a maximum aperture of f4.5. This is very slow compared to the faster, larger apertures of f1.8 on the Canon 85-mm lens, f2.0 on the 100-mm lens, f2.0 on the 135-mm lens, and f2.8 on the 200-mm lens. Indeed, each of the non-zoom lenses I've mentioned here is significantly more expensive than the 75-200-mm zoom. But they are also much brighter lenses that allow you to use them earlier in the morning and later in the evening, thus extending your productive shooting time every day. Of course, faster aperture (such as f2.8) zoom lenses are available but at a higher price. (For reference, my 80-200-mm f2.8 "L" autofocus lens cost more than $1,000!)

Many photographers feel that changing fixed-focal length lenses is a time-consuming burden to be avoided. On the contrary, the entire procedure can be completed in fifteen to twenty seconds once you are experienced at swapping lenses — hardly time consuming. (One small tip to help expedite your lens changing and protect your equipment: use spare front and rear lens caps as well as body caps.)

Fast-Glass, Extra-Bright (and Expensive) Lenses

When it comes to capturing the clearest, sharpest, most colorful shots on slide film, most sports, fashion, action, and magazine photographers turn to the equipment manufacturer for premiere lenses that feature extra-large apertures, exquisite glass, and often phenomenal price tags. Designated as "L" lenses (for luxury) by Canon, APO (for apochromatic) by Minolta, and ED (for extra-low dispersion glass) by Nikon, these are the finest lenses made. They have the special ability to focus not only the image but also

the three primary colors of light. This ability removes virtually all problems of color fringing and, therefore, increases both resolution and contrast. Bigger, sharper enlargements can be made from slides or negatives, and photos reproduced in magazines have more sparkle or life to them. While I don't shoot generally at the largest maximum aperture these lenses make available, I focus and compose with extreme ease thanks to their extra brightness. These apochromatic lenses come in a variety of focal lengths ranging from ultrawide angle to super telephoto along with zooms as well.

The two drawbacks of fast-glass lenses are their extra weight (due to the larger elements of glass) and the premium price you must pay. Since I'm a professional photographer and I need the best

People play a vital role in running, servicing, and maintaining the locomotives and rolling stock of North America's railroads. Take advantage of any opportunity to make photos of rail workers. The candid approach works well, although you can use longer lenses if you don't want your subjects to know you are photographing them.

(Opposite page) At Proctor yard in Minnesota, hostler helper Ron Van Dell fills the sand box of a Duluth, Missabe & Iron Range SD18, one of seven such EMD locomotives in the ore-carriers fleet. Canon T90, 85 mm, Fujichrome 50, 1/125th, f6.7

(Above) In Green Bay, Wisconsin, the engineer of GB&W No. 305, an Alco RS20M, peers out of his cab while switching cars on August 14, 1989. Canon T90, 135 mm, Fujichrome 50, 1/250th, f4.5

equipment I can obtain for a variety of assignments, I can justify the expense (gulp). But can you? If you think you can, congratulations; you'll get a tremendous amount of enjoyment using these fine optics. If you think not, don't despair. Fine railroad images can be made with comparatively ordinary lenses. However, I do recommend you buy and use the best fixed-focal length name brand (Canon, Nikon, Minolta, Olympus) lenses you can afford.

Starting Off: Prime Lenses

A prime selection of three lenses and one camera could serve you quite well. Combinations such as 28-mm, 50-mm and 135-mm lenses, or 35-mm, 85-mm and 200-mm lenses, or 50-mm, 135-mm and 300-mm lenses cover many of the basic needs of railroad photographers. Later on, the addition of one more lens and one more camera body brings you into the realm of owning and using a camera system.

Medium Format Equipment: An Introduction

Cameras that use 120 or 220 size roll film are medium-format cameras. They are available in three styles: rangefinder, twin-lens reflex, and single-lens reflex; four formats: 6x4.5 cm, 6x6 cm, 6x7 cm and 6x9 cm; and are made by nine major manufacturers including Hasselblad, Rollei, Plaubel and Exacta.

The chief advantage of using these roll-film cameras instead of (or along with) 35-mm cameras lies in their ability to produce a larger negative or transparency. Such transparencies and negatives require significantly less enlargement to obtain a desired print/page size, thereby retaining greater apparent sharpness, definition, and tonality. If your goal is to produce the finest-grained, highest-quality color or black-and-white blow-ups (11" x 14", 16" x 20", 20" x 30" or larger) you must consider using roll film cameras. Or, you may be like me and simply wish to use medium format cameras to photograph large-scale scenes such as massive railroad bridges or vast trainscapes with great detail — detail that would be lost between the grains of today's most advanced 35-mm films.

An additional benefit found in several models of roll-film cameras (including two of the seven that I recommend) is their interchangeable film backs. These allow you to change instantly from one film stock to another, even in mid-roll. One such back is the Polaroid Film Holder, which allows you to make a test exposure and review a processed proof in sixty seconds. It's an indispensable tool for evaluating lighting placement for nighttime locomotive shots or for making critical decisions regarding composition.

However, the advantages of medium-format equipment do not come without compromise. Medium-format cameras are larger (and in some cases much heavier) than 35-mm equipment, cost more, and use excellent, but slower, maximum aperture lenses. Also, many models do not have built-in light meters. Roll-film cameras are slightly more difficult to operate and, therefore, slower to use. Although the available 120/220 film stocks are varied, you may not be able to obtain all of your favorites. Another disadvantage of 120 film is the

reduced number of exposures per roll: 15 with 6x4.5-cm cameras, 12 with 6x6-cm cameras, 10 with 6x7-cm cameras, and 8 with 6x9-cm cameras. That's considerably less than the 36 exposures you're probably accustomed to. (The number of exposures per roll is doubled with 220 film, but 120 is more readily available.) However, don't let these drawbacks discourage you from looking into the purchase of medium-format equipment. With patience, some practice, and selective use, roll film cameras and lenses can help you produce stunning results with phenomenal detail and clarity.

Recommended Medium Format Cameras

Listed here are seven somewhat diverse roll-film cameras that meet my criteria for railroad photography. They are lightweight (five of the seven models), relatively inexpensive, durable, and use rectangular film formats. Though 6x6-cm cameras are very popular, I dislike their square format, which does not allow you to make maximum use of the full negative or transparency. My favorite seven include:

The Bronica ETRSi (6x4.5 cm/ 2 1/4" x 1 3/4"), a

single-lens reflex camera with interchangeable film backs for 120, 220, 35-mm, and Polaroid film. Includes autoflash control with through-the-lens metering when used with Metz flash units; eight interchangeable lenses; interchangeable prisms and focusing screens; motor drive, winder, and manual speed grip; and a full system of accessories. This camera is the most durable and economical of the three 6x4.5-cm SLR camera systems made today. (Pentax and Mamiya are the other manufacturers.) The price for a camera with waist-level finder, 120 back and 75-mm f2.8 Zenzanon lens is approximately $1,450.

The Fuji GS645S Professional (6x4.5 cm/ 2-1/4" x 1-3/4"), a compact, double-image rangefinder camera with a fixed 60-mm f4 EBC Fujinon-W lens, bright viewfinder, and three-point LED meter and single-stroke film advance. The diminutive size and light weight of the GS645S, along with its modest price of $570, make it an excellent camera for those just entering into medium format photography.

The Pentax 6x7 (6x7 cm/ 2-1/4" x 2-3/4"), an SLR that looks and handles like a giant 35-mm camera. It

Ultrawide-angle lenses — 14-mm, 17-mm, 20-mm, and 24-mm focal length—are often useful to separate foreground and background elements. These lenses also provide tremendous depth of field from mere inches to infinity.

At Norfolk Southern's Fort Wayne, Indiana, yard, eastbound train No. 306 makes final preparations for departure on a sunny September weekday. Canon T90, 14 mm, Fujichrome 50, 1/60th, f11.5

features an electronically timed shutter; uses both 120 and 220 film; has a rapid-wind film advance; accepts first rate Pentax lenses; and has numerous interchangeable focusing hoods, prisms, and accessories. It is the least expensive 6x7-cm medium-format system available. A camera body, prism, and standard 105 f2.4 lens costs roughly $975.

The Mamiya RZ67 (6x7 cm/ 2-1/4" x 2-3/4") combines the versatility of the earlier RB67 and advanced electronics for fast, simple, and easy operation. An SLR, the RZ67 features a revolving back for a near-instant change from horizontal to vertical (and vice versa). It accepts eighteen superb Mamiya Sekor lenses, and its available interchangeable film backs include 120, 220, 6x6 cm, 6x4.5cm and Polaroid. It also has an extensive selection of other accessories. Although the most expensive and heaviest 6x7-cm camera, the RZ67 is an excellent camera system for those who like to shoot locomotives from a tripod in both day and night settings (primarily because of the larger format and Polaroid proofing capability). A camera body, focusing hood, 120-film back, and 110-mm f2.8 lens sell for around $2,400.

The Fuji GW670II Professional (6x7 cm/ 2-1/4" x 2-3/4"), a lightweight, quick-handling rangefinder camera that provides professional performance from its non-interchangeable 90-mm f3.5 EBC Fujinon lens. It also provides 120/220 film capabilities, two-stroke film advance, flash sync at all shutter speeds, shutter speeds from 1 to 1/500th of a second, and time setting. The GW670II has no built-in light meter and costs a reasonable $750.

The Fuji GW690II Professional (6x9 cm/ 2-1/4" x 3-1/4") and the Fuji GSW690II Professional (6x9 cm/ 2-1/4" x 3-1/4")are two similar cameras that have nearly identical features as those of the previously mentioned Fuji GW670II. The primary difference is the larger 6x9-cm format. The GW690II uses the fixed 90-mm f3.5 EBC lens and sells for $750. The GSW690II uses the Fujinon-SW 65-mm f5.6 wide-angle lens and costs $850.

Note: Light readings for medium-format cameras not equipped with built-in meters can be made in two ways: take a reading using your 35-mm camera and compensate for any film speed/exposure differences, or use a handheld exposure meter (discussed in the film and light chapter).

If you are considering getting into medium-format photography seriously, I highly recommend that you purchase *The Medium Format Manual* by Michael Freeman (Fireside Books, 208 pages, $15.95). It is a comprehensive guide to selecting and using roll-film cameras and equipment that is chock full of comparison charts, instructions, and more than 250 photographs and diagrams.

Lens Shades

With few exceptions, camera lenses come with or are designed to accept lens shades. Use them! They are essential because they keep the sun from striking the front element of your lens. This causes flare and subsequent image degradation. (Image degradation is any factor that detracts from the optimal quality that could be expected from clean well-designed cameras and lenses.) A rigid type of lens shade can also protect the front element of your lens from damage or destruction if the lens is dropped. Besides, lens shades are inexpensive. I use them on all my lenses all the time. I am convinced that my regular use of lens shades is an important contributing factor to my ability to consistently create sharp, clear, and attractive photographs.

Useful Filters

Used selectively, photographic filters provide numerous benefits that include color correction, image enhancement, and special effects.

Color correction filters are used to warm up or cool down the color temperature of light falling on your subject. On overcast days, using cooler daylight films like Ektachrome, may require you to use such filters as the 81A, 81B, and 81C. In varying degrees each adds more warmth and affects the final depiction of a scene. More extreme, but worth considering, are the 85, 85B, and 85C.

Image enhancement filters consist of three types: UV (ultraviolet), skylight, and polarizers. The UV filter absorbs ultraviolet light rays, which sometimes make outdoor photos hazy and indistinct. If you find it necessary to photograph during the middle of the day this filter could be useful.

The skylight 1B filter reduces the excessive blue cast that occurs frequently in open shade and under a clear blue sky. This filter has a minor magenta color tint that adds slight warmth to the overall color balance. When used at a 90-degree angle to the sun, polarizing filters eliminate glare and reflection from subjects such as water, windows, and so on, and increase color saturation. Thus, blue skies can be rendered darker and contrast can be improved in a given scene. Check with your local photography store to determine if you need a standard polarizer or circular polarizer for your specific camera model.

Special effects filters can be fun toys; however, they can lose their appeal easily and become

When time permits and you use a second camera, you can create dramatically different photos of the same subject from a significantly different perspective. Here are two photos illustrating that point.

(Opposite top) On Florida's East Coast, Florida Tri-Rail train No. 213 rolls to a stop at Boca Raton station to pick up commuters during the evening rush hour. This shot was made to emphasize the passengers, platform, and engine front. Canon EOS-1, 80-200 zoom at 200 mm, Fujichrome 50, 1/250th, f5.6

(Opposite bottom) The second shot, made one minute later, reveals a lot more of engine No. 805, an F40PHL built from a GP40 frame and an F45 car body, as it eases the train out of the station enroute to Miami. Canon T90, 20 mm, Fujichrome Velvia 50, 1/250th, f5.6

Standard lenses of 45, 50, and 55 millimeters are good choices for general train photography. Their large maximum apertures of f1.8, 1.4, and 1.2 make them especially useful in low light.

Sunset on one of the world's most heavily used single-track railroads —The Orin Line of Burlington Northern and Chicago & North Western in Wyoming. Another train of empties approaches Shawnee Junction, destined for a refill at one of the massive Powder River Basin coal mines. Canon F-1, 50 mm, Fujichrome 100, 1/125th, f1.4

superficial if they are overused. One type of special effect filter that deserves a place in your camera bag is the graduated neutral density filter. This filter has a colorless dark-tinted top tapering down to clear glass. It can be used on bright days to even out the exposure differences between the sky and the lower half of your composition. This filter helps if the locomotives or trains you are shooting have a dark paint scheme (for example, Norfolk Southern, Southern Pacific, or Rio Grande) or are extremely dirty. Graduated color filters are just like graduated neutral density filters except that they are color tinted. The two most popular choices are tobacco and blue. Their main role is to add color to an otherwise uninteresting sky.

As with lenses, select the best filters you can afford. I use the B+W brand and am very happy with

cables that are designed for newer equipment. For true remote operation use a Quantum Radio Slave 4, which will provide up to 250 feet of wireless control.)

When selecting a tripod, disregard descriptive words like small, lightweight, or cheap. Instead, think stability. If you don't have a good steady tripod, you won't have sharp photos, which means you could be a very discouraged photographer. The smallest tripod I recommend is the Uniphot Tiltall. I have used one for fourteen years, and it handles 35-mm and medium-format cameras with ease. It has a maximum extension height of 70 inches, a closed length of 30 inches, and weighs just more than 6 pounds. The price is $130. I also use a much larger and more expensive Bogen location/studio tripod, the 3051 with 3047 head. It's rock steady, even when supporting super telephoto lenses. Bogen also makes several smaller, less expensive versions that seem like excellent, sturdy choices. Benbo tripods also are well made and feature a unique design that allows their legs to adjust to a variety of angles for use on uneven ground.

Carrying Your Gear: Camera Bags and Cases

You need a camera bag from the moment you acquire your first camera, lenses, and accessories. Dozens of companies offer a variety of types, colors, sizes, and shapes. Some of the more respected name-brand manufacturers of camera bags include Billingham, Fotima, Tenba, and Tamrac. I use the Lowe-Pro Magnum, which is a large, soft, padded nylon bag for carrying the majority of my 35-mm equipment, film, filters, and other necessities. A Domke F-1x — a large, soft, unpadded cotton canvas bag — carries my two 6x9 cameras, 120 film, and accessories. I utilize the compact Domke F-3X bag (same type as F-1X) for odds and ends and handheld flash equipment. If I really want to travel light, I'll use the F-3X to carry one camera, a few lenses, and eight or nine rolls of film.

Although they are significantly heavier, you might consider a camera case for carrying your equipment, especially if you work primarily out of your car and only go field trekking occasionally. Hard camera cases offer excellent protection against equipment damage during shipping, storage, and transporting. The Tundra Sea King series of all-weather cases are waterproof, dustproof and crushproof. Made of strong, durable ABS plastic, they provide the optimum safekeeping for your valuable equipment.

Cleaning Your Photo Equipment

Dust, dirt, and grit are the bane of all photographers on the road or at home. It's imperative to keep your camera and lenses clean at all times. Besides causing image degradation, particles on or inside your camera can cause equipment malfunctions or, just as bad, scratches on your film. Routine cleaning takes only ten to twenty minutes per session and should be performed as necessary, depending upon the amount you use your equipment and your shooting region. When I'm at home in the Northeast, I need to clean my gear only about once every four weeks. However, in the deserts of the Southwest, cleaning may be

their performance. However, limit the use of filters because extra layers of glass can cause flare, halation and loss of sharpness. Don't use filters for lens protection. That's the job of the lens cap.

Tripods

Along with cameras and lenses, a good sturdy tripod plays a vital role in the railroad photographer's outfit of equipment. A tripod helps you steady a long lens, assists in setting up and composing with both 35-mm and medium-format cameras, and allows you to explore the worlds of long exposure and nighttime photography. Additionally, you can shoot with two cameras: using one hand held and the other mounted on a tripod and fired simultaneously by remote. (The least expensive method is to use a 15-foot pneumatic release on older style cameras or the remote release

35mm / 15/16" x 1 7/16", Canon EOS-1 w/50mm lens

6x4.5cm / 2 1/4" x 1 3/4", Bronica ETRSi w/75mm lens

6x7cm / 2 1/4" x 2 3/4", Mamiya RZ-67 w/110 mm lens

6x9cm / 2 1/4" x 3 1/4", Fuji GW690II w/90mm lens

The advantages of medium format cameras with their larger transparencies or negatives are apparent when the 6x4.5cm, 6x7cm and 6x9cm formats are compared to the diminutive 35mm frame. Medium format transparencies and negatives require considerably less enlargement to make big display prints or large color separations for magazine covers, center spreads, calendars, and posters. Notice that the focal length range of lenses is slightly different for each film format. For example, a 50-mm lens provides a normal perspective in 35 mm, but a wide angle perspective in 6x7 and 6x9. These four photographs were made of restored Erie caboose C-177 at the Whippany Railroad Museum in Whippany, New Jersey. All exposures were made on Fujichrome Velvia 50, 1/125th, f8

A significantly greater amount of detail can be recorded onto a medium format transparency or negative, resulting in greater apparent sharpness in the finished photograph. This is especially important when you shoot large-scale rail scenes and you want to see all the subtle intricacies of your subject.

An Amtrak AEM7 crosses the Susquehanna River on the Northeast Corridor at Havre de Grace, Maryland, with westbound Metroliner No.119 in tow. The date is October 25, 1990, at 4:52p.m.
Fuji GSW690II Professional, 65 mm, Fujichrome Velvia 50, 1/250th, f5.6

essential as often as every other day.

The procedure is simple. The only requirements are a large, flat surface, lens tissue and lens cleaner, a can of Dust-Off or other environmentally safe type of compressed air, two washcloths (one dry and the other wet but not dripping), and a small soft brush.

First wipe the exterior surfaces (but not the glass) of each lens and camera body with the damp cloth; then wipe again with the dry one. Be sure to clean the insides and outsides of your lens and body caps as well. Next, blow any dust particles from the front and rear lens elements with compressed air, being careful to keep the can upright. (Should you accidentally tip or turn over your compressed air can, blow the nozzle clear of any propellant before directing the air stream towards your equipment. This prevents the application of messy propellant residue to your camera or lens.)

Then, if necessary, use your lens tissue and cleaning fluid to remove fingerprints, smudges, or watermarks from the elements. Work in a gentle circular motion. Blow out any dust particles from the camera body, but be extremely careful to avoid directing an air stream at the shutter curtain and the mirror, because damage could result. Use a small, soft brush to remove dust from the mirror's surface. If you use a camera with a removable viewfinder and/or focusing screens (such as the Canon F-1 or Nikon F-3), blow them free of dust at this time also. Be sure to clean the camera's viewfinder eyepiece with compressed air and the lens cleaner as necessary. Filters should receive attention now, too. Last of all, thoroughly clean the interior of your camera bag with a damp cloth to remove extra dirt or grit.

Maintaining Cameras and Lenses

Due to mishap or routine wear and tear, lenses and (primarily) cameras need professional repairs through the years. The obvious choice for servicing is one of the factory repair stations operated by each individual camera manufacturer. Their locations usually are listed in your camera's instruction manual. Alternatives to these in-house facilities can often be found closer to home. I've used two independent camera repair shops with excellent results: Strauss Technical in Washington, D.C., and

Ultrawide-angle lenses play a significant role in railroad photography. The fisheye type, however, is only occassionally useful because of its odd distortion and gimmicky look.

Here's an example of this distortion. On the Northeast Corridor at Deans, New Jersey, a westbound AEM-7 with trailing Metroliner coaches passes under a catenary support on May 6,

1990. Canon T90, 15 mm, Fujichrome 50, 1/750th, f2.8

Nippon Photo Clinic in New York City. Both facilities repaired my obsolete equipment that no longer was being serviced by the Canon factory station. For facilities in your area, check the directory/classified ad section of *Shutterbug* or *Photo District News*.

Where to Purchase Photo Equipment

Ideally, the best place to buy photo equipment is from a trustworthy, well-stocked camera store offering sound advice, reasonable prices, and a friendly, courteous sales staff. If you have a store in your area that fits these criteria, shop there. If you don't, I'd like to recommend two excellent sources for photographic equipment.

Ken Hansen Photographic in New York City is one of the largest, most reliable camera stores in the world. Catering to advanced amateur and professional photographers, the store carries an extensive selection of all major 35-mm and medium-format camera systems, along with light meters, filters, tripods, and so on. Used equipment in exceptional condition can also be purchased there.

The nationwide leader in mail-order sales of photography equipment is Calumet Photographic of Bensenville, Illinois. Its 200-page catalog is full of all the goods and accessories you'll need in your quest for picture perfection. Products range from large-format cameras to darkroom equipment, from filters and tripods to chemicals and film.

Alternatives to Buying Equipment — Renting

The high cost of buying specialty cameras, exotic super telephoto lenses, and powerful lighting equipment can be distressing economically. Fortunately, renting is an alternative to buying equipment.

Over the past four or five years, renting has become popular among professional photographers who need certain high-ticket equipment for a special assignment or shooting session. Advanced amateurs can take advantage of renting as well. If you live near a major city or can receive United Parcel Service (UPS) shipping, you can rent cameras, lenses and lighting equipment for a day, weekend, week, or month at a fraction of the purchase cost. For example, the Canon 400-mm f2.8 "L" manual focus lens sells for about $4,500 plus tax. A daily rental is $75. The special weekend rate is $75 (from Friday 1:00 pm to Monday 10:30 am), and the weekly rate is $225. In some cases, the rental fee can be deducted from the purchase price if you decide to buy. As a word of caution, I advise anyone renting equipment to shoot a test roll before embarking on any photo expedition. Rental equipment is available through numerous photo supply houses listed in *Photo District News*.

Film and light

While the cameras and lenses you choose determine the mechanical parameters of making a good railroad photograph, the film you use defines the look and feel of your creative efforts. There are a number of factors to consider when choosing film types, but initially there are only three: whether to shoot black-and-white film for prints, color negative film for color prints, or color transparency film for slides. Each choice has unique advantages.

Black-and-white film is the least expensive to shoot, especially when you process and print your own work. Also, all the railroad magazines (and most books) have a greater need for black-and-white shots. So, your chances of getting published are better in black and white if that is one of your goals.

Color negative film has a broad exposure latitude, which allows more room for exposure error. Also, color prints are immediately ready for viewing without the need of a darkened room and slide projector.

Color slides provide the truest color, allow easy storage, and are capable of being projected. Additionally, color slides are the standard for color photo reproduction in magazines and books. With slides, you also have the option of making prints at a later date. By far, slide film (also called transparency, chrome, or reversal film) is the most popular among railfan photographers. All of the text and captions in this book refer to the use of color transparency film.

The features of slide film that affect significantly the final outcome of your images — and ultimately your satisfaction — are film brand, film speed, and (in some instances) film type (either amateur or professional). Let's take a closer look at each of these features.

Film Brand

A number of film manufacturers offer a wide variety of slide films that appear to be suitable for general all-around photography at first glance. This is, however, an incorrect assumption since many are too fast, made from motion picture stock, or just outdated technologically. Rely on the major manufacturers such as Agfa, Fuji, and Kodak. They produce film consistently to the strictest tolerances and quality control standards, thereby assuring you of optimal results.

Film Speed

Commonly known as ISO (International Standards Organization), film speed is a numerical value that designates a film's sensitivity to light. The smaller the ISO number, the more light a film requires; the higher the ISO number, the less light required to record a given scene. To simplify matters, film is referred to as slow speed (ISO 25 to 64), medium speed (ISO 100 to 200), and high speed (ISO 400 and up). As film speeds go up, so does the cost and the amount of grain visible in your pictures. This is due to the increased quantity of light-sensitive silver halide crystals in each roll. For photographing trains, film speeds of ISO 50 to 100 are best. They provide more pleasing and accurate color and tighter grain patterns, which yield sharper images. ISO 200-speed films are useful and sometimes necessary when shooting in less than ideal light. If it is so dark and gloomy that you need a 400 ISO film, then switch to black-and-white film. Rarely do high-speed color films give acceptable results upon critical review.

Amateur versus Professional Film

Agfa, Fuji, and Kodak offer their films in amateur and professional versions. Amateur film is intended to sit on a camera store shelf for several months to a year before reaching its peak maturity with regard to color rendition. Professional film, on the other hand, is manufactured and shipped at the height of its color ripeness and is designed to be exposed and processed immediately. It produces the most accurate color. In addition, professional film has a true ISO compared to the inaccurate sensitivity ratings sometimes encountered with amateur versions. Of course, you don't have to be a professional photographer to use

From time to time you may need a higher-speed film than you usually carry or shoot with. If so, "push" your E-6 type film to a higher ISO and have your processing lab compensate accordingly (for further explanation, see text). The main advantages of pushing are extra speed and increased contrast. The drawbacks are more pronounced grain in the image and the extra cost of special handling by the lab.

On the last day of February, 1991, traffic on Santa Fe's Seligman Subdivision was hampered by a heavy, wet snow. At the signal bridge at mile post 336 in East Flagstaff, Arizona, five GP60Ms in red- and-silver Warbonnet paint scheme made their way downgrade with an eastbound Hyundai Stack train. Canon F-1, 300 mm, Fujichrome Velvia 50 pushed to 200, 1/250th, f4.5

Though pushing the effective speed of a film one or two stops is fairly commonplace, a +3 stop push is unusual. Certain situations may warrant the procedure, however. At 7:07a.m. on a foggy November morning in 1990, I shot Fujichrome Velvia 50 rated at ISO 400. The extra speed was required for two reasons: the extremely low light level and the need for a fast shutter speed (1/250th of a second).

The fast shutter speed was needed to freeze the motion of westbound Delaware and Hudson's DHT-9 doublestack train passing Conrail's Corning, New York, yard lead on the Southern Tier Line.

Canon F-1, 300 mm, Fujichrome Velvia 50 pushed to 400, 1/250th, f4.5

professional film. However, read the upcoming section on purchasing, storing, and carrying your film, since professional film stock needs more careful handling than its amateur counterpart.

Film: The Least Expensive Component

Film is fairly inexpensive compared to all the other expenses associated with train photography (equipment costs, accessories, gas, food, and lodging). Don't pick one film over another because it costs 35¢, 45¢, or a $1.00 less per roll. This is false economy. Use the best film that works for you regardless of the price, the one that you feel has the best color, grain, and contrast.

Also don't skimp with film when you are trackside, anticipating some heavy traffic, and your camera's frame counter reads 32, 33, or 34 exposures taken. Either finish the roll by taking a few quick shots of your friends or your car, or simply rewind the exposed film and then reload. You'll be ready to capture all the action with a fresh roll of film rather than having to reload in the thick of things (possibly missing the best shots). Besides, each individual frame of processed slide film costs only about 45¢. So don't hesitate to reload.

Slide Films: Which Are Best?

You have dozens of color transparency films from which to choose. To aid in your search for the best film, I've listed the eight choices that I feel are the best for shooting trains. You'll need to do your own testing and evaluation, since each film has its own subtle variations and characteristics, but all are first-rate films capable of producing excellent results. My eight selections, in order of preference, are as follows:
1. Fujichrome 50 Professional (RFP-135-36)
2. Fujichrome 100 Professional (RDP-135-36)
3. Fujichrome Velvia 50 Professional (RVP-135-36)
4. Kodachrome 64 Professional (PKR-135-36)
5. Ektachrome 64 Professional (EPR-135-36)
6. Ektachrome 64-X Professional (EPX-135-36)
7. Ektachrome 100 Plus Professional (EPP-135-36)
8. Kodachrome 200 Professional (PKL-135-36)

All of these films are professional stock, assuring the utmost in image quality. All but the two Kodachrome films are E-6 type films that can be processed in three to four hours in hundreds of labs throughout the United States and Canada. All the films (with the exception of Kodachrome 200) are available in both 35-mm and 120 roll-film sizes. (Note: Although Kodachrome 25 is an excellent film with the finest grain, it was not included in this suggested list because its very slow speed makes it impractical for the all-around needs of railroad photography.)

Slide Films: My Preference

Kodachrome has long been the standard of railfans. Based on my experience, however, I feel the three Fuji films named above are superior. From 1975 to 1985, I shot thousands of rolls of Ektachrome and Kodachrome film, obtaining what I would now consider to be fairly good results. In 1985, I shot my first 20 rolls of Fujichrome 50 film side by side with

Slow-speed films range from ISO 25 to ISO 64, including Fujichrome 50, which is my favorite film. It provides crisp, accurate color, minimal grain, and excellent saturation and contrast. Currently, about 40 percent of all my images, including my railroad photos, are made on Fuji 50. Roughly 35 percent of my work is done on Fujichrome Velvia and 25 percent on Fujichrome 100.

A prime example of Fuji 50's great color can be seen in this photo of Ontario Northland's X-121 passenger train, taken at Northbay, Ontario, on August 23, 1989. These two ex-Trans European Express (TEE) locomotives are now used only as control units. Canon T90, 35 mm, Fujichrome 50, 1/250th, f6.7

Medium-speed films range from ISO 100 to ISO 200 and aren't as colorful or sharp as slow-speed films. Additionally, grain is often more apparent. But when you need the extra speed, you've got to use them. When might a 100- or 200-speed film be required? When photographing on less than ideal days, when a fast shutter speed like 1/500th of a second or faster is necessary, and when you use slow (small maximum aperture) telephoto lenses. Unless you are confronted with an extremely rare set of circumstances, it's seldom advisable to shoot with any film beyond ISO 200 if you want good colorful images.

(Below) After uncoupling his train, a Conrail crewman directs his engineer to backup the set of light engines so he can throw the switch for the fueling and sanding racks at Conrail's Selkirk, New York, yard. Canon F-1, 400 mm, Fujichrome 100, 1/500th, f5.6

(Right) During a heavy August 1987 downpour, Denver & Rio Grande Western GP40-2 No. 3104, a GP40, and an SD40-2 slog along the 4th subdivision near Sage, Colorado, with train No.179 in tow. Canon F-1, 300 mm, Fujichrome 100, 1/250th, f2.8

twenty rolls of Kodachrome 64 while on vacation in southern Utah. The results with the Kodachrome were quite nice, but the results with the Fuji 50 were absolutely stunning. As a result, I haven't used anything else since.

Fujichrome 50 and 100 possess a high degree of color accuracy and excellent color saturation combined with a slightly warm color balance that enhances any outdoor scene, including those with locomotives, people, and details. Both films have exceptional grain structure with crisp details and sharpness. Additionally, this pair of films look best when exposed normally for their true respective film speeds.

The key highlights of Fujichrome Velvia are the film's superlative fine grain and very high color contrast — finer than other ISO 50- or 64-speed film made. In bright sunlight, Velvia's colors are saturated with brilliant highlights. On flat cloudy days, Velvia's warm color balance and high contrast produce respectable color slides when some other

manufacturers' films fail. On overcast days, when Velvia's ISO 50 speed is insufficient for me to shoot at 1/250th of a second or faster, I "push" Velvia (expose it at a higher ISO rating and compensate during processing) to ISO 100 or even ISO 200 with very good to excellent results.

Purchasing, Storing and Carrying Your Film

Regardless of the brand or type of film you choose, there are several important considerations you should keep in mind when you buy, store and transport your unexposed and exposed film. Try to find one or two local camera stores that carry your film preference and buy your film there regularly. If you'd like to try shooting professional film, find a photographic film stock house in your area. If there's no stock house nearby, find one elsewhere in your region and have your order shipped by Overnight UPS. Stock houses receive direct refrigerated shipments of the time- and heat-sensitive pro films from the manufacturers every couple of weeks. They

then store the film in large coolers. Try to anticipate how much film you'll need for each trip, then buy that amount, plus several reserve rolls, before you leave. Don't assume you will find your exact film type being sold in some small-town drugstore along the way.

Keep all of your film (with the exception of what you carry in your camera bag) refrigerated at home until you are ready to use it. However, be sure to allow 2 1/2 to 3 hours for the film to warm up to the current temperature before removing it from the protective canister or foil wrapping. Otherwise, condensation may form, possibly causing uneven exposure.

When I'm on the road for an extended shooting trip, I carry about 30 rolls of 35-mm film in my main camera bag along with additional film placed in clear-bottomed plastic storage bins with tight-fitting lids. These bins are kept in a cooler (filled one-quarter of the way with ice) in the cargo area of my car. This provides me with chilled and fresh batches of film every few days. My exposed film (with the leaders **33**

wound back all the way into the cassettes) is placed in the original film canisters and then into the storage bins in the cooler. Therefore, it receives the same protection from high temperatures as the unexposed film. (Put 120 film into multiple zip-lock bags and then into the bins and coolers).

(Note: Keep your storage bins above the ice level by placing them on top of a couple of six packs of soda or some empty bins. This keeps the film storage bins out of the water when the ice melts.)

All of these procedures may seem like a pain in the neck. But it's one more factor that you control, which ensures the quality of your finished images. If you are planning a week's trip or longer, it's smart to take this extra precaution with your film.

Another critical factor that may affect your film is x-ray. When you travel by commercial aircraft, both your check-in and carry-on luggage will go through an x ray machine. No matter what the quantity, hand carry your unexposed (and exposed) film. Insist that it be searched by hand, not machine. This eliminates the risk of accidental exposure (called fogging) by an uncalibrated x-ray machine or untrained operator. Arriving at the airport ten to fifteen minutes earlier than usual will allow you the extra time. Using the clear film containers and plastic bins will further expedite your inspection.

You don't have to be paranoid about film handling. But do take every opportunity you can to ensure that your film is cared for properly.

Film Processing

When it comes to color transparency film, there are only two types of processing labs: E-6 for Agfachrome, Ektachrome and Fujichrome, and K-14 for Kodachrome. Naturally, the processing lab you choose depends on the film you shoot. In either case, the lab plays a major role in how well your slides turn out. The two most important elements are a need for a nonbiased color balance and care in the processing and mounting stages. Poor workmanship can result in off-color and scratched or stained frames, which if once ruined are ruined forever. The closest or most convenient lab may not be the best choice. To find a good lab in your area, call several professional photographers listed in your yellow pages to get their recommendations. After four or five calls, you should have a good idea of who or who not to use.

Because of the intricate and specialized process required for Kodachrome film, there are only a few

other labs besides the Kodalux network to pick from, all of which are located in major metropolitan areas. Several can be found by reading *Photo District News*. These independent color labs are not only an alternative to the Kodalux service but also offer other Kodachrome processing services such as "pulling," "pushing," and clip tests. Pull processing is used when you have intentionally or accidentally shot a roll of film (in this case Kodachrome) at a slower ISO speed than normal. (Example: Kodachrome 200 at ISO 50.) Push processing is used when film is shot at a higher speed than normally rated. To push or pull a roll of film, first label it for the ISO you desire, set the ISO on the camera accordingly, and shoot away. Then have your lab process the film according to your instructions. The maximum range of push/pull is usually plus or minus two to three f-stops. Pull processing flattens contrasty lighting (sharp

Photographers discuss natural light in three ways: quality, color, and direction. Hard light is a quality. It describes conditions on clear days when the sun is brightest and the shadows most harsh. This light is especially bad from midmorning to midafternoon. Though it would be ideal to shoot earlier or later, sometimes you'll be in an irresistible situation and will shoot anyway. Here are two examples of hard light. They were shot at the same location and at roughly the same time of day, but four years, two hundred yards, and about 180 degrees difference in shooting angle separate the two shots.

(Opposite page) It's 12:33p.m. on March 5, 1991, on SP's Sunset Route at Mescal, Arizona. The El Paso-to-Tucson drag passes an old coaling tower that used to feed steam locomotives their supper. Canon EOS-1, 80 to 200 zoom at 135 mm, Fujichrome Velvia 50, 1/500th, f4.5

(Above) In December 1987 a westbound freight trundles past, unimpressed by the history and romance of the place. Canon F-1, 400 mm, Fujichrome 100, 1/500th, f8

Soft light is encountered on hazy, foggy, smoggy, or partly overcast days when the sun's rays are diffused and softened. This, in turn, lowers the contrast between highlights and shadows, making it possible for you to photograph more of the subtle colors and shapes in a scene.

(Opposite top) The sun's rays haven't cut all the way through a morning fog on Chicago & North Western's West Iowa Subdivision. An eastbound TOFC train bears down on a curve near Arion, Iowa. Canon F-1, 300 mm, Fujichrome 100, 1/500th, f4.5

(Opposite bottom) On a hot and hazy summer evening in 1988, multiple Chessie/CSX locomotives await fueling and sanding at Cumberland, Maryland. Canon F-1, 400 mm, Fujichrome 100, 1/500th, f5.6

(Above) Block operator Walter Kowal flags an eastbound Conrail train and prepares to hand up a track warrant at MP 162 on the Boston and Albany Line at the New York-Massachusetts state line on a sultry June day in 1988. Canon T90, 200 mm, Fujichrome 50, 1/250th, f4

Because the majority of color films are balanced for daylight use in sunny conditions, completely overcast days present two problems: lower light levels and cooler color temperatures. These lead to bland color photographs. But you have a few alternatives: be selective and don't shoot at all, shoot black -and-white, shoot color and accept the results, shoot warmer films like Fuji 50, Fuji 100, Fuji Velvia, Ektachrome 64X, or Ektachrome 100x, or use a color correction "warming" filter. I tend not to shoot at all or to accept what I get, though I'd recommend Fuji Velvia pushed to ISO 100/200 for anyone constantly confronting inclement weather.

(Above) At Stuyvesant, New York, one of Amtrak's six EMD FL9s powers No. 48, The Lakeshore Limited, east along the Hudson River towards New York City on a dismal October 19, 1990. The FL9s are unique because they can operate in dual modes — diesel/electric or 600-volt DC for third rail connection in the city. Canon T90, 300 mm, Fujichrome Velvia 50 pushed to ISO 100, 1/250th, f4.5

(Opposite page) On a snowy day in March 1989, Amtrak No. 8, the eastbound Empire Builder, is over two hours late as its engineer grabs the train orders at Soo Line's Grand Crossing Tower in La Crosse, Wisconsin. The tower, which has since been razed, guarded the crossing of Soo Line's Tomah Subdivision with BN's 3rd Sub Mainline. Canon T90, 24 mm, Fujichrome 100, 1/250th, f4

contrasts of tone, as between light and dark areas), and pushing increases contrast in flat light. Both affect color balance.

In clip tests (used when an entire roll of film is shot at the same exposure) a few frames at the beginning are clipped off and processed. Then, upon your inspection, the lab will either push, pull, or process normal the remaining roll of film. This service is usually used by studio photographers but could be useful for photographing nighttime rail scenes. (Be aware that seldom, if ever, is the clip made between frames, so you will lose one frame). Clip tests and push/pull processing are available for E-6 films, too.

Light

The type of weather and light you encounter trackside on any given day is purely a matter of luck. Not only do train photographers need to be concerned with the amount of light but also its direction and quality. From sunrise to sunset, we are presented with a nearly infinite variety of lighting conditions that slowly evolve throughout the day as the earth's atmosphere changes. Because color daylight films are designed and balanced for use in sunlight, it is important to understand how they react in different illumination.

Some of the more common terms relating to the quality and direction of light include:

Hard light. The type you encounter on clear, cloudless days. The direct sunlight is extremely bright and contrasty, casting very pronounced or hard shadows on the ground. The light of midday is often too harsh to make attractive photos.

Soft light. A flattering light, found on sunny days with high, thin clouds and on days when the air is hazy or smoggy and the sun's rays cannot penetrate as strongly. Shadows are visible but much less obvious than in hard light. Also, soft light has a wraparound lighting effect as opposed to the very directional look of hard light.

Cold light. The term often used to describe a day with a completely overcast sky and no apparent sunlight, resulting in slides with a cool or cold blue cast. Shadows are nonexistent. Heavy color correction is recommended unless you are shooting for a unique color effect. For example, when shooting in winter time, you may want a bone-chilling look.

Warm light. The golden or orange light typically found at sunrise and sunset when the sun's rays filter through haze, smoke, and smog. The light is often quite soft and yields photographs that are the most visually and psychologically appealing. Warm light is often found on hot, humid days in the summer.

Front lighting. Describes the angle of light falling onto the front of a locomotive or train facing directly into the sun. This over-the-photographer's-shoulder light direction has been the recommended guideline for years and provides excellent results time after time.

Side lighting. The term for light striking a subject from a 90-degree angle to the camera. This produces an interesting half-highlight, half-shadow look that's quite exciting and acceptable in many instances since it enhances the illusion of three dimensions.

Back lighting. The effect created by light coming from behind a locomotive or other subject. At sunrise and sunset when the sun is low on the horizon, this

lighting can be used to produce dramatic silhouettes. At other times, light may bounce off of a hillside or building back onto the front of the subject thus illuminating detail, texture, and color. The direct sunlight highlights the overall shape or outline of your subject. Though back lighting can help you create some very exciting images, it is often a difficult light to meter correctly.

All of these lighting conditions (with the exception of cold light and the harsh light of midday), contribute to the production of interesting and dynamic photographs. Knowing which type of light yields the best shots and which light looks the worst is a major asset to your photographic success. Study and observe the subtleties of light every day, taking note of its direction, color, intensity, and quality as the day progresses. Watch how the shadows from trees, telephone poles, and signs fall on the ground. They'll not only indicate the direction of the sunlight but also its type — hard or soft light.

Working with Light

I try to be selective of the light conditions I work in when I'm chasing trains. For me, early mornings and

late afternoons are the ideal times to be out on the mainline. I start my day one to two hours before sunrise so I can drive to the location I've selected previously for the first light of day. I'll shoot routinely for three or four hours, taking advantage of morning light.

I rarely do much shooting midday when the high sun is the least flattering. Instead, I use that time to scout locations for the afternoon or following morning and to get supplies (food, fuel, ice for film, and so on.) Sometimes, I'll use midday to travel to another area or simply to rest. Then, in early afternoon, I'll be trackside again, taking advantage of the last three or four hours of daylight, shooting until a half hour or so after the sun has set.

I'm not a fair-weather photographer who is afraid to brave the elements to get a shot of a certain train or locomotive. But then again, I know from experience when the weather and light are so bad that I shouldn't bother to step outside. Heavy cloud cover is the worst scenario. About the only things you can do are shoot black-and-white, scout around, or go home. (As an example, I once cut short an extended trip to the Southwest after having driven all the way

Because of the warm golden light that occurs when the sun is low on the horizon, early mornings and late afternoons are ideal times to be out and about photographing trains.

(Opposite page) A storm has passed through North Platte, Nebraska, and has cleared the air. Two Union Pacific SD40-2 hump engines bask in the sunshine atop the hump at UP's Bailey Yard. Canon F-1, 300 mm, Fujichrome 100, 1/250th, f3.5

(Above) Five Burlington Northern SD40-2s guzzle from a fuel tender while drawing a loaded coal train past West Haire siding on the jointly owned and operated Orin Line in Wyoming's Powder River Basin. Canon T90, 135 mm, Fujichrome 50, 1/250th, f2.8, polarizing filter

to Texas through eight days of continuous rain with more precipitation predicted.)

It is essential to have some sunlight to produce acceptable color slides, even if it is only from a few clouds reflecting and bouncing the light around. I relish the bright, clear sunny days, as do most photographers; but if there is some sunlight, you'll also find me shooting in intermittent showers, fog, mist, and snow. These atmospheric elements can add a lot of feeling or mood to a railroad scene and provide the opportunity to make photos that have a distinct appearance.

The time of day and type of weather you shoot in not only add great variety to your railroad slide collections but literally make or break the overall impact of each individual image. Be selective. Take advantage of "nice" light, and your efforts will be rewarded.

Light — Making a Correct Exposure

Four key elements come into play every time you take a light reading prior to photographing a train: the film's ISO, the relative brightness of the scene, the shutter speed you use, and the f-stop you select. I like to think of all four of these variables as being somewhat like the elements found on an engineering slide rule. Change one number here, and three other variables may be affected. The film speed (ISO) is the first element, and it remains a constant factor during the course of 36 exposures. The relative brightness varies throughout the day and directly affects the shutter speed selected. Since we want to freeze the action in our moving train photos regularly, we routinely use fast shutter speeds (1/250th, 1/350th, and 1/500th of a second). This in turn dictates the f-stop required.

Also of consequence in making a correct exposure is the area in a scene you meter off of and the type of metering pattern your camera uses. Almost all 35-mm cameras have built-in light meters (called reflective meters) that measure the amount of reflected light bouncing off the subject toward the camera. Light meters are insensitive to color and only measure light reflectance in shades or percentages of gray. Various manufacturers calibrate their meters differently, but almost all consider an 18 percent reflectance as the standard for a correct exposure. Numerous "real world" items reflect 18 percent and can be used to take your readings from when trackside. Grass, dark or wet concrete, a dark dirt road surface, gray ballast, and weathered wood are all suitable targets. It's especially important to be

Front lighting comes over the photographer's shoulders and strikes the subject, be it a train or locomotive, from a mostly frontal angle.

(Top) Climbing directly into the sun between Chamiso and Mescal, Arizona, Amtrak No. 1, the April 16, 1989, edition of the Sunset Limited, is only 45 minutes off schedule on its journey from New Orleans to Los Angeles. Canon F-1, 400 mm, Fujichrome 100, 1/500th, f4.5, tripod

(Bottom) Two of Central Michigan's four GP38ACs, all rebuilt from GP40s, usher train No. 702 south on its Bay City to Durand run on a snowy morning near Zilwaukee, Michigan. The vantage point is the Interstate 75 overpass. Canon F-1, 50 mm, Fujichrome 50, 1/250th, f6.7

(Opposite page) With Horace Mesa looming in the background, a Santa Fe freight rolls west on the Gallup Subdivision near Grants, New Mexico. Canon EOS-1, 300 mm, Fujichrome 50, 1/250th, f4.5

Side lighting provides an interesting alternative to front lighting by producing longer shadows that often add depth to a scene or subject. Take care, though, to avoid obscuring too much of your train or locomotives.

(Above) Along a cactus-lined roadbed, Southern Pacific stack train AXAVT506 bears down on Cochise, Arizona, on a sunny weekday morning in March 1991. Canon EOS-1, 80-200 zoom at 200 mm, Fujichrome 50, 1/500th, f4

(Below) At Boston's North Station at rush hour in November 1989 a Massachusetts Bay Transportation Authority F40PH moves out with three carloads of commuters. Note the grids that protect the front windshields and engineer from projectiles. Canon T90, 300 mm, Fujichrome 50, 1/350th, f4.5

(Opposite page) Under the wires on the Northeast Corridor north of Princeton, New Jersey, an AEM7 draws 11,000-plus volts to race its six Metroliner coaches along at 125 miles per hour. Canon T90, 20 mm, Fujichrome 50, 1/750th, f3.5

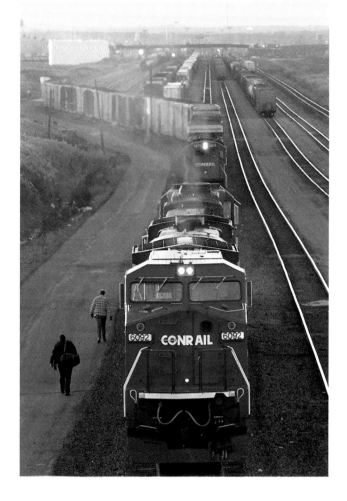

Because of problems relating to lens flare and inaccurate exposure, backlighting is the most difficult light in which to photograph. The results, however, can be extremely dramatic, so it's almost always worth trying a few shots.

(Left) On a crisp New England morning in Selkirk, New York, weary crews are dismounting, and hostlers are shuttling engines around Conrail's enormous classification yard. Canon T90, 300 mm, Fujichrome 100 pushed to 200, 1/125th, f4, tripod

(Opposite top) In the early morning light a Southern Pacific Westbound TOFC train winds its way through the immense horseshoe curve at Caliente, California, at the west end of the Tehachapi Mountains. On the siding (far left), a work train's engines fire up for a day of track maintenance on the mountain grades. Canon F-1, 200 mm, Fujichrome 100, 1/500th, f5.6

(Opposite bottom) South of Gillette, Wyoming, on the Orin Line that serves the majority of the Powder River Basin coal mines, Burlington Northern No. 92, a Seattle-to-Houston intermodal, rolls along at twilight behind a silhouetted LMX B39-8. Canon T90, 24 mm, Fujichrome 50, 1/30th, f4

sure of the exact areas from which you meter. Most older cameras have an averaging meter pattern, which reads the light reflected back from a very broad area and averages the highlights, midtones, and shadows simultaneously. Newer camera models like the Canon EOS-1 and EOS-10S have four highly sophisticated multiple-metering patterns to choose from: six-zone evaluative metering, center-weighted averaging, partial metering, and spot metering. All of these are available to you at the turn of a dial. The partial and spot patterns are especially useful for making critical exposure readings. Partial metering is an intermediate pattern covering 5.8 percent of the picture area and is extremely helpful in backlit or contrasty situations. Spot metering covers only 2.3 percent of the field of view and is invaluable whenever you need to pinpoint the precise area of exposure interest. I use the partial and spot meter patterns almost exclusively on my T-90 and EOS-1. Rarely do I employ the averaging pattern to take light readings. Making a correct exposure for the train, especially the locomotives, is always my primary goal. Averaging patterns can get confused by bright skies, fields of snow, and dark forests, thus giving you a radically underexposed or overexposed image.

If you use a camera that only has an averaging meter pattern — or a medium-format camera with no meter at all — you may want to consider an auxiliary light meter. The Minolta Spot Meter F makes precise, one-degree spot readings and looks somewhat like a sci-fi movie ray gun. It displays digital-exposure information both in the viewfinder and on a liquid crystal display located on the meter's side. Small and

lightweight, it comes with a belt pouch and costs approximately $440. You can get a similar spot reading effect, though not nearly as conveniently, with an older model camera equipped with an averaging meter pattern. Simply mount your longest telephoto lens, take a reading and switch back to your shorter focal length lens. Just remember to set the aperture accordingly on the shorter lens.

There are two other valuable tools that can provide assistance when you're trying to make exact light readings. The first, and least expensive, is the 18 percent gray card. Gray cards were designed years ago for studio photographers who needed a standard of reference when preparing to photograph a myriad of subjects on a variety of backgrounds. Outdoor photographers can use gray cards, too. They are indispensable when shooting wintertime rail scenes since other midtone targets may not be available. You simply hold the card out at arm's length, fill the camera's viewfinder frame with the card, and take a reading while allowing the same light as that striking your subject to illuminate the gray card. Some testing is required to learn how your film and camera's meter will work with the gray card. Several photographic suppliers make 18 percent gray cards, including Kodak and Unicolor. I use the plastic Unicolor version, called "The Last Gray Card," because it is virtually indestructible, scratchproof and fade resistant. Prices vary depending on the manufacturer and size of the gray card you select, but they range from $8 to $16.

Another important exposure aid is the handheld incident light meter that measures the amount of light falling onto your subject. Many photographers

The key highlights of Fujichrome Velvia are its superlative fine grain — finer than any other ISO 50- or 64-speed film made —and high color contrast. In bright sunlight Velvia's colors are extremely saturated and brilliant. On less-than-ideal days Velvia's warm color balance and high contrast produce unrivaled color slides.

(Above) On Union Pacific's Lynndyl Subdivision in Utah, eastbound LAOG and its grab-bag assortment of cars rounds a bend at MP 682 on March 15, 1991. Canon EOS-1, 80-200-mm zoom at 135 mm, Fujichrome Velvia 50, 1/250th, f5.6

(Opposite page) Conrail SEEL2 bound for Elkhart, Indiana, departs Selkirk, New York, yard behind a pair of CSX locomotives and one Conrail unit. Canon EOS-1, 300 mm, Fujichrome Velvia 50, 1/250th, f4.5

Several medium format cameras do not have built-in light meters, and on several models a meter is optional. So how do you determine the correct exposure? Use an auxilliary light meter or use your 35-mm camera's meter.

On New Jersey Transit's Boonton Line, a westbound Metro-North GP40FH-2 shuttles a NJT passenger train across the Hackensack River on "DB Draw," a deck girder and thru-truss swing bridge. Pentax 6x7, 90 mm, Fujichrome 100, 1/250th, f4.5, exposure determined with a Canon T90 and 50-mm lens.

rely on them exclusively for accurate light measurements. Incident readings are taken with the meter's spherical diffuser directed toward the camera position. As you did with the gray card, make sure that you are not taking a reading in the shade when your subject is in direct sunlight. This will result in an overexposed slide. Minolta makes two nice lightweight incident meters: the Autometer III and the Autometer IV F. They are virtually identical except that the IV F model can also be used to take electronic flash readings from 1/500th to 1 second. Continuous light readings of up to thirty minutes can be made with both meters. Exposure data is shown digitally on a liquid crystal display. Both are excellent choices for daytime and nighttime railroad photography, with the IV F having a slight advantage because of its flash-reading capability.

All the high- and low-tech camera features and auxiliary light metering tools can leave you uncertain at times whether the recommended light reading is correct. What to do? Bracket. Bracketing means making a series of varied exposures of the same subject or scene to assure a successful result. This is almost always accomplished by changing the aperture and leaving the shutter speed alone. For example, if your meter recommends an exposure of 1/250th of a second at f5.6, you could make a bracket for f4.5, f5.6, and f6.7 (1/2 stop over, normal, and 1/2 stop under). The range in f-stops that you bracket from the suggested normal reading depends on how uncertain you are that the reading is correct. Another deciding factor is how important the shot is to you. If you hike two miles in a blizzard to photograph the California Zephyr emerging from a tunnel and you are stymied as to the exact exposure, then bracket to guarantee that you get the shot.

Bracketing is such a common practice among photographers that the major camera manufacturers are now producing cameras with automatic bracketing available at the push of a button. My EOS-1 has autobracketing and it can be employed even when the camera is used in the manual exposure mode. Sure, bracketing wastes some film, but when it's required, it's better than coming home empty handed.

Planning a train watching trip

Now that we have covered the basics of cameras, lenses, film selection, and light, it's time to plan a trip. For me, this process is usually a gradual one. Often it starts on a boring evening while sitting in front of the television, or as my mind wanders from some of the more tedious tasks of my work. The next thing I know I'm flipping through my well-worn Handy Railroad Atlas dreaming of some enchanting subdivision or hot spot 200 — or even 2,000 — miles away.

Research is one of the most rewarding and enjoyable aspects of railfanning and railroad photography, so be sure to invest this valuable time preparing for your trip. There are essentially four places to get good, in-depth information about the particular railroad or region you plan to visit: reference books, railroad magazines (both current and back issues), railroad videotapes, and employee timetables.

Reference Books

There are literally hundreds of books on railroads currently in print, and new books are released every month. The subjects range from broad overviews of huge railroad systems and historical titles to books documenting the detailed accounts of minuscule shortline operations. Most can be found (or ordered) at well-stocked model railroad shops, many of which are also great places to gather information.

If you live in a remote part of the country, just look through the ads (and book reviews) in Railfan & Railroad or Trains magazines, and let your fingers do the walking. A few of the more generic and useful books I'd recommend are:

• The Train Watcher's Guide to North American Railroads by George H. Drury (Kalmbach Books, 228 pages, $14.95), considered the "bible" by many railroad enthusiasts. This handy softcover book features important, basic information about more than 140 railroads in the United States, Canada, and Mexico.

• American Shortline Railway Guide by Edward A. Lewis (Kalmbach Books, 320 pages, 4th edition, $18.95), an up-to-date directory of small, regional and industrial railroads operating in the United Sates.

The book includes detailed locomotive rosters, providing engine numbers, builders, models, and dates built.

• The Historical Guide to North American Railroads by George H. Drury (Kalmbach Books, 424 pages, $24.95) provides interesting historical data pertaining to 160 abandoned or mergered railroads.

• The Contemporary Diesel Spotter's Guide Update by Jerry A. Pinkepank and Louis A. Marre (Kalmbach Books, 336 pages, $18.95) features facts, details, and photos of the vast fleet of diesel and electric locomotives operating in North America. This book is a must if you want to learn to identify the various makes and models you'll encounter.

• Compendium of American Railroad Radio Frequencies, 12th edition, by Gary Strum and Mark Landgraf (Kalmbach Books, 208 pages $16.95) lists railroad frequencies for nearly every railroad in the United States.

• 1993 Official Locomotive Rosters by James W. Kerr (DPA-LTA Books, 122 pages, $19.95), an annually updated pocket-size listing of 734 Canadian, Mexican, and United States rosters, representing more than 31,000 diesel, electric, gas, and steam locomotives. Included is the model number, year built, and horsepower.

• Train Watcher's Guide to Chicago by John Szwajkart (240 pages, $15.50).

Train Watcher's Guide to St. Louis by John Szwajkart (192 pages, $11.50).

Train Watcher's Guide to Kansas City by John Szwajkart (184 pages, $15.25). These three books (each with an accompanying three-color foldout map) are a tremendous aid when railroad hunting in these cities and their surrounding areas. Each contains numerous photos and minimaps and information on dozens of rail-related points of interest, especially towers, yards, and interlockings.

Magazines

Every month a wealth of railroad information emerges from a handful of excellent magazines catering to rail enthusiasts. Accompanied by exciting and sometimes exotic photographs, their feature articles are excellent sources for planning your next

---

Location has an important effect on how well you capture the essence of a railroad or subdivision. An ideal setting will feature interesting flora, fauna, structures, or terrain unique to the region.

The steeple of St. Mary's Catholic church in Little Falls, New York, reaches for the heavens as Conrail's TV-201 rounds Gulf Curve on October 18, 1991. Fifty-one years earlier 31 passengers and railroad personnel died when the New York Central Lake Shore Limited derailed at this spot. Canon EOS-1, 80-200-mm zoom set at 150 mm, Fuji Velvia 50, 1 350th, f4.5

trip. They can also be the inspiration for a jaunt.

• *Extra 2200* South has nationwide coverage of locomotives: rosters, rebuilding notes, and details of engines sold or scrapped.

• *Pacific Rail* News contains some of the best up-to-the-minute news on railroads west of the Mississippi, plus several feature stories and close-ups on specific locales.

• *Passenger Train Journal*, as its name implies, publishes features and news items about United States and Canadian passenger operations and equipment.

• *Railfan & Railroad* prints nationwide and Canadian news and feature stories with numerous color and black-and-white photos. Its "Camera Bag" column addresses many contemporary railroad photography topics. Coverage tends to favor the eastern United States.

• *Railpace* contains news and feature stories about railroad activities in the Northeast and eastern Canada. Each issue highlights in great detail a specific area or city accompanied by driving directions and maps.

• *Trains* regularly provides news, features and historical stories on a national and international level. Its "Hot Spots" column provides a two-page, in-depth look at busy train-watching spots across the country. Coverage tends to focus on the Midwest and West.

Interestingly enough, model railroad magazines often have detailed backgrounds about real railroad operations in various regions of the country and can prove useful.

Back issues of all these magazines are worth their weight in gold if they contain the information you need. Look for them at model railroad shops, model railroad shows, railroad flea markets, or purchase them directly from the magazines.

Railroad Videotapes

These are another good source of background information about a specific railroad or region. The last few years the railroad videotape business has realy taken off, and there are a number of good producers.

Pentrex has established itself as the unequivocal leader, with dozens of top quality tapes of its own and dozens more by other producers, including some early, steam-footage videos. Tapes by Video Rails, WB Video, Hopewell, Greg Scholl Video, Green Frog, and several other smaller producers round out the selection.

(Above) Deep in the Sonora Desert east of Gila Bend, Arizona, Southern Pacific's Gila subdivision threads its way through cholla- and saguaro-covered mountains. On the point of the LADAF (Los Angeles to Dallas Forwarder) is SSW Cotton Belt 8043, a GE B40-8. Canon F-1, 200 mm, Fujichrome Velvia 50, 1/250th, f4

(Opposite page) Along the banks of the Columbia River, a westbound Burlington Northern train of autoracks and containers on flat cars crosses a fill at Horsethief Lake State Park, Washington. In the background are a portion of the huge Basalt Cliffs that form the Columbia River Gorge. Canon F-1,

200 mm, Fujichrome 100, 1/500th, f4.5

Photographs of trains going away from the camera can often be more interesting than approaching shots of the same train. If you're at the right place at the right time, you might be able to get an exciting image of one train meeting another as well.

(Top) On Montana Rail Link's mainline at Greycliff, Montana, eastbound train No. 192 (farthest from the camera) waits in the hole while a westbound hotshot flies by. Both lead units are leased **GE LMX B39-8 locomotives.** Canon T90, 300 mm, Fujichrome 100, 1/250th, f4.5

(Bottom) Conrail's TV-7 hustles its all-TOFC train towards Waterloo, Indiana, running almost four hours ahead of time on the 31-hour Boston-to-Chicago schedule. Canon F-1, 800 mm, Fujichrome 100, 1/500th, f8, tripod

If at all possible, preview the tapes you are interested in before purchasing them. Sometimes quality is shoddy, and a few tapes are just plain boring. Fortunately, most are worthwhile.

Railroad Employee Timetables

These are the handbooks carried by railroad operating employees. Their size and formats vary, but the basic principle is the same: to provide concise, mile-by-mile information about stations, sidings, lengths of passing tracks, speed limits, special speed restrictions, and often locomotive rosters as well. Since you will find often that names of railroad locations do not exist on highway or topographic maps, timetables are essential to pinpoint the vicinity of a train you hear on the scanner. In some cases, timetables include track profiles that illustrate grades. This is useful when you want to find locations where the trains have to work uphill.

Timetables also list exact locations of "talking" dragging equipment or hot box detectors, which warn train crews by radio of trouble with their train (and potentially impending danger). Fortunately for us, they function regardless of the train's condition. They announce the railroad, location, and (again, depending upon the system) train speed, axle count or direction of travel. In many cases, the engineer is required to acknowledge the radio message; in so doing the engineer states the train's number/symbol.

You can obtain employee timetables from a few sources. Simply write to a railroad and ask for one, or inquire at crew-change points about their availablity. You'll see employee timetables for sale at model railroad shops and shows, at railroadiana shows, and at flea markets. Or you can contact collectors or dealers.

Don't be afraid to purchase or use timetables that are two or three years old. In many cases you or I would never notice the differences between outdated and current versions. Also, don't confuse timetables with train schedules. Freight and passenger train schedules list when trains run, unlike employee timetables, which usually don't contain schedules.

Maps

When my wife Susan and I first started traveling to photograph trains several years ago, we made the mistake on one or two occasions of not bringing along a detailed map showing the tracks and terrain of the area we were railfanning. Our frustration grew every time we stopped in a book or sporting goods store and were politely told, "Sorry, we don't carry maps" or when the maps we did find did not show railroads. Now, along with a radio, research material, timetables, cameras, and film, we carry dozens of maps of various types and sizes. They include:

• Handy Railroad Atlas (Rand McNally, 64 pages, $14.95). This is a must. It's a quick and easy way to get an overview of the rail lines in the various states. But highways or terrain features are not included.

• The 1993 Road Atlas (Rand McNally, $7.95) These are the familiar, large maps of the highways with some terrain features for the fifty states and the Canadian provinces. Although the road atlas omits railroads, it is useful and gives an accurate overview of highways and secondary roads. Plus, it lists each state's Department of Tourism offices with addresses and phone numbers (many of which are toll-free numbers). Usually, these offices gladly provide literature about their states at no cost, along with large state maps that often show railroad tracks.

State Atlases

Two publishers currently produce highly detailed maps presented in a page-by-page format and similar in size to Rand McNally's Atlas.

• DeLorme Mapping prints excellent color atlases of Alaska, California (two editions, Northern and Southern/Central), Colorado, Florida, Idaho, Illinois, Maine, Michigan, Minnesota, New Hampshire, New York, North Carolina, Ohio, Oregon, Pennsylvania, Tennessee, Vermont, Virginia, Washington, and Wisconsin.

• County Maps publishes black-and-white state atlases for Arkansas, Florida, Indiana, Kentucky, Michigan, North Carolina, Ohio, Pennsylvania, South Carolina, Tennessee, West Virginia, and Wisconsin.

Sizes vary from atlas to atlas, but all are roughly 1:150,000 scale size (commonly referred to as 150K), where one inch equals approximately 2.3 miles. These atlases show railroad tracks, landmarks, major roads, and highways, as well as small dirt roads. Keep a fluorescent marker on hand to highlight the rail lines and other points of interest because the type size and rail lines are extremely small and thin. Prices range from $10.95 to $14.95, depending on the atlas.

Topographic Maps

The United States Geological Survey (USGS) sells first-class topographic maps of the United States. There are two useful sizes for rail photographers: the 1:500,000 scale size shows states, and one inch equals approximately 8 miles. For example, the state of Arizona map measures 47" x 53" — surely big enough to decorate a wall in your office or den. But folded up to reveal only portions of the state, it is handy enough to use in the car.

For a more in-depth view of a smaller area, however, the USGS offers 940 maps covering the continental United States in the 1:250,000-scale size (one inch equals approximately 4 miles), measuring 22" x 32". For trainchasing over a large area (120 miles or more) you will probably need several of the 250K-scale maps. More detailed (smaller scale) maps are available, but I highly recommend the 1:250,000 size for almost all situations where a state atlas is not available. The 250K-scale maps sell for $4.00.

Scanners

Next to photographic equipment, a scanner is the most expensive and important investment you need to make to enjoy train watching and railroad photography. A scanner is a multiband receiver radio that scans multiple channels for communications on amateur, business (including railroads), and public safety frequencies. Developed in the late 1960s, these continuous-scanning radios have truly come of age during the last decade by utilizing state-of-the-art

Instead of making another run of the mill roster shot on your railroad outings, look for interesting or unusual backdrops to create environmental portraits of locomotives.

Alongside a towering grain elevator in Kansas City, Kansas, a pair of Soo Line SD40s and a Chessie System EMD brethren idle while awaiting the next call of duty. Canon F-1, 20 mm Fujichrome 100, 1/125th, f4

microprocessors. Today's synthesized or programable scanners are versatile and easy to use. Simply turn on the radio, punch in the desired railroad's frequency, assign a channel, and repeat until you have programmed all the desired frequencies or the scanner's channels are filled. Depending on the model, capacity ranges from 10 to 200 channels.

For your first scanner, I would recommend a handheld portable unit because of the greater flexibility it offers compared to a mobile unit mounted in your car. Later on, you might like to purchase a mobile radio. Take note, however: In most states it is illegal to possess or operate a scanner in your motor vehicle. While I'm sure these laws are intended to avert criminal use, be forewarned of the possible consequences.

There are several important features found in most handheld and mobile scanners that I feel are essential:

Priority. A scanner's ability to allow you to select and sample one favorite channel and to override all other calls while still scanning.

Delay. A two-seconds pause after a transmission that allows you to hear both sides of a conversation on one channel.

Channel banks. These allow you to program your frequencies into groups or banks of frequencies (usually twenty at a time). For example, you may want to monitor aircraft on channels 1-20, railroads on channels 21-40, or fire departments on channels 41-60.

Flexible rubber antennas (handheld scanners only). Tough and hard to break, "rubber duckies" are the only antennas to consider if you are an active trainchaser. While telescoping metal antennas work a bit better, they break easily and often damage the tops of handheld units if dropped.

Both mobile and handheld scanners can be purchased through bigger electronics stores and the Radio Shack chain. Another excellent source is Scanner World USA in Albany, New York, which claims to be the largest dealer of scanners in the world. It carries several of the top brands, including Cobra, Regency, and Uniden Bearcat, as well as all

the necessary accessories such as antennas, nicad batteries, chargers, and so on. I have been very pleased with the quality of both my Cobra SR-11 and Regency HX-1500 scanners.

The three best sources for finding the proper railroad frequencies to program into your scanners are Kalmbach's *Compendium of American Railroad Frequencies*, *Train Watcher's Guide to North America*, and *American Shortline Railway Guide*. You'll also find new and updated frequency listings in several of the railroad magazines, accompanying articles in *Railfan & Railroad*, *Railpace* and *Trains*.

Hot Spots

Following is a descriptive list of twenty of the more interesting railroad locations and regions I have traveled to and photographed. Obviously, there are dozens, perhaps hundreds, of equally impressive areas throughout North America. However, those listed here are favorites because they feature two key ingredients essential to a productive photo outing: Spectacular or unique scenery along with easy

Permission to enter and photograph in railroad yards is often impossible to obtain. If you are enterprising, you can still get good shots at the yard's limits. Many of the larger yards like Conrail's facility at Selkirk, New York, Chicago & North Western's Proviso yard in Chicago, and Norfolk Southern's Bluefield, West Virginia, yard are spanned by public bridges that make great shooting perches. In most cases topographical maps and state atlases will show enough detail to indicate such crossings or adjacent hillsides.

(Left) Under the watchful eye of a car inspector, a tiger-striped GP-50 brings outbound No. 60, an all-TOFC train, through Burlington Northern's Galesburg, Illinois yard. (Top) On the north side of Galesburg yard is the engine fueling and sanding facility. Both shots were made from an overpass spanning the yard. Canon F-1, 300 mm, Fujichrome 100, 1/500th, f4

(Bottom) Nestled in the hills and hollers at the extreme southern part of West Virginia, Norfolk Southern's Bluefield yard is often found choked with multiple unit coal trains. But on March 30, 1988, the yard is empty except for this train departing for the docks at Norfolk. The photograph was shot from an overpass at the far east end. Canon F-1, 200mm, Fujichrome 100, 1/250th, f6.7

Keep a watchful eye for trackside structures and railroad and highway signs bearing the name of a certain location or town. With a little ingenuity they can be incorporated into your compositions, making the storytelling of photography a little easier to follow.

(Above) Four Burlington Northern SD40-2s usher an assorted consist of bulkhead flat cars, boxcars, and empty covered hoppers past a grain elevator near Lind, Washington, in 1987. Canon T90, 28 mm, Fujichrome 50, 1/250th, f6.7

(Right) On October 13, 1988, a pair of Chicago & North Western SD60s and two UP engines team up to guide HSELX012 into Caballo mine in Wyoming, where its 110 coal cars will be loaded. Canon T90, 24 mm, Fujichrome 50, 1/250th, f6.7

(Opposite page) Saluda Hill in the far western part of North Carolina is, as the sign says, steep. Its maximum grade is 5.1 percent. Norfolk Southern mixed freight train No. 171 is seen here making its second and last trip of the day up the grade after doubling the hill on November 17, 1988. Canon T90, 28 mm, Fujichrome 50, 1/250th, f5.6

accessibility, and a line (or lines) that is heavily traveled and that offers a variety of traffic, such as unit coal, mixed freight, intermodal, grain trains, and perhaps passenger service as well.

Altoona, Pa. Located in central Pennsylvania, Altoona is the core of activity on Conrail's busy Harrisburg-to-Pittsburgh main line. It features the Juniata shops (Conrail's only locomotive back shop), nearby Horseshoe Curve, and roughly sixty trains every 24 hours (including four Amtrak runs). Although the Allegheny Mountains are small by Western standards, they are still a tough obstacle. Many trains require helpers both ascending and descending the mountain grades just west of Altoona. Numerous overpasses and pedestrian walkways make downtown Altoona a good shooting area. Horseshoe Curve, the tunnels at Tunnel Hill and Gallitzin (along with several interlocking towers) and the helper base at Cresson are also great locations. Altoona is an enjoyable area to visit year round but especially during the colorful fall foliage.

Bluefield, W.Va. Bluefield is located on the eastern edge of West Virginia's coal-mining region and is Norfolk Southern's Pocahontas Division headquarters. Eastbound export coal and westbound empties keep the former Norfolk & Western double track territory very busy. Frequent curves and tunnels (along with numerous mine spurs) make this region prime territory for rail photographers (although it can be somewhat inaccessible in places). The yard in downtown Bluefield is often choked with loaded coal hoppers. Also, locomotives are fueled, sanded, and supplied here. Several bridges spanning

63

the tracks make shooting easy and fun. Try traveling here during the spring or fall.

Cajon Pass, Calif. The near-continuous parade of Amtrak, Santa Fe, Southern Pacific and Union Pacific traffic, combined with the grueling grades between the San Gabriel and San Bernardino mountains, makes this one of the most famous train watching locations in North America. Located a short distance north of San Bernardino, Cajon Pass runs alongside Interstate 15, but the accessible areas are located off State Rt. 138. Due to the close proximity to the Los Angeles Basin and the subsequent problems with smog, try to visit Cajon Pass during the clearer winter months, early spring, or fall.

Cheyenne - Laramie, Wyo. The stark but beautiful desolation of southern Wyoming creates an impressive setting for the scores of trains linking the eastern and western segments of the Union Pacific system. Some fifty trains a day shine the rails between Cheyenne and Laramie (which includes Sherman Hill, the highest point on the transcontinental railway), offering much diversity for photos. The scenery includes large, colorful rock outcroppings and tall pines. Often trains are run in groups of three or four (called fleeting), and the action can be fast and furious. Winter photography here is challenging due to constant winds, so a spring or summer visit would be more enjoyable. Comfortable accommodations are available in both Cheyenne (also served by the Burlington Northern) and Laramie.

Columbia River Gorge, Wash./Ore. Forming the state border between Washington and Oregon, the Columbia River Gorge is in itself a region of great scenic beauty. Burlington Northern tracks on the north shore and Union Pacific tracks on the south are set against the blue water and tan bluffs, creating a kind of wonderland for the visiting photographer. Train activity flourishes with grain, double stack, and Amtrak traffic over both hosts' rails. Other noteworthy features include BN's Celilo Bridge crossing the Columbia at Wishram, Wash., and UP's huge Hinkle, Ore., yard further east. Spring, summer, and fall are the best bets, but if the cold doesn't bother you, try a winter trip.

Duluth, Minn./Superior, Wis. Situated on the extreme western end of the Great Lakes, the small, friendly cities of Duluth and Superior are active railheads for the Duluth, Missabe & Iron Range Railroad, BN, CNW, and Soo Line. CN's subsidiary railroad, the Duluth, Winnipeg & Pacific, operates nearby as well. Most interesting, however, are the trainloads of taconite (used to make steel) that the

DM&IR moves from the mines in the north to the huge 1,000-foot-long ore docks on Lake Superior. Gigantic grain elevators also dot the waterfront, and large ships regularly come and go during the busy spring, summer, and fall months. Neighboring Proctor, Minn., hosts the DM&IR's large sorting yard and locomotive facilities.

Fraser and Thompson River Canyons, British Columbia. The southern portion of the province of British Columbia in western Canada is the home of two spectacularly beautiful river canyons. Running primarily north to south, the narrow river banks are traversed on one side by Canadian National and on the other by Canadian Pacific. Each railroad runs more than twenty trains per day; passenger service is provided by VIA Rail triweekly on Canadian National. You'll see trains hauling lumber, containers, and coal, not to mention grain trains resplendent in their unique "Wheat Board of Canada"

Once you find a location with reasonable train traffic and a vantage point you like, shoot there at different times of the day.

(Opposite page) On the afternoon of November 1, 1990, I found an out-of-service bridge straddling Conrail's Chicago-to-New York main line near Weedsport, New York, west of Syracuse. After photographing several trains, I made this photo of Conrail's SETO (Selkirk, New York, to Toledo, Ohio) heading west into a glorious sunset at 4:43 p.m. Canon EOS-1, 300 mm, Fujichrome 50, 1/250th, f5.6

(Above) Feeling that this new found hot spot would be equally productive in the morning, I returned the following day and shot eastbound Amtrak No. 48 *The Lakeshore Limited* at 7:20 a.m. Since I wanted the cornfield as a foreground, I stood a mere 40 feet from where I made the Conrail shot. Canon EOS-1, 300mm, Fujichrome Velvia 50, 1/250th, f4

paint schemes. Fall is the best time to visit this region because of copious precipitation during the rest of the year. The area is so pretty, however, I suggest trying your luck anytime. Comfortable accommodations can be found in Hope and Kamloops, British Columbia.

The Hudson Highlands, N.Y. Forty miles north of metropolitan New York is an area along the majestic Hudson River called the Highlands. Bracketed by the Newburgh-Beacon Bridge to the north and the Bear Mountain Bridge to the south, each side of the river experiences considerable train activity. On the east bank, Amtrak operates up to twenty Empire Corridor trains per day mixed in with approximately twenty-five Metro North commuter trains during summer daylight hours. On the Hudson's west shore Conrail runs eight to ten daytime trains moving freight between New Jersey

yards and its Selkirk, N.Y., yard just south of Albany. A variety of interesting photo opportunities are available on both sides of the river, including Conrail's tunnel under West Point, the mix of old and new locomotives on the passenger side, and breathtaking vistas throughout the area. All of this makes the Highlands enjoyable year round.

Kingman-Seligman, Ariz. Situated in the northwestern portion of Arizona, Santa Fe's Seligman Subdivision handles thirty to forty trains per day, including Amtrak's *Southwest Chief.* All eastbound traffic must make a 220-mile sustained climb from Needles, Calif., (elevation 520 feet) to Riordan, Ariz., (elevation 7,335 feet) near Flagstaff. Constantly changing weather conditions in the mountains and mesas serve as a dramatic and expansive backdrop for exciting images. The tracks traverse interesting rock cuts and canyons around Kingman and further

to the east. The Seligman Sub is great to visit all year but especially during fall, winter, and spring. The summers are extremely hot.

La Crosse, Wis. The east bank of the Mississippi River in southwestern Wisconsin is skirted by the Burlington Northern's double track main line linking Chicago and Minneapolis. High bluffs overlooking the wide great river, countless picturesque spots, and numerous trains create an outstanding setting worthy of exploring throughout the year. The best access is from East Dubuque north to Prairie Du Chien and on up to La Crosse, which is a BN crew change point (also the best place to stay). Soo Line has a river crossing here, and its tracks head north on the west side of the Mississippi but are not as accessible or scenic. On several stretches of the river, it's possible to get BN trains and grain-laden barges in the same photo.

Many old railroad depots, coaling towers, round houses, and other buildings still stand trackside. They are remnants of a bygone era. Some are abandoned, some restored, and some still serve duty. These structures make impressive images, but it's also exciting to include contemporary equipment passing by, creating an interesting juxtaposition of old and new.

(Left) On a bitterly cold day in 1989, some 80-plus years after the Durand, Michigan, station was built, Amtrak train No. 365, the westbound *International*, prepares to highball on Grand Trunk tracks. During the golden years, Durand Station served over a dozen passenger trains per day, a far cry from the one eastbound and one westbound Amtrak service of today. Canon F-1, 24-mm, Fujichrome 50, 1/250th, f6.7

(Right) Amtrak train No. 353, *The Lake Cities*, on its daily Toledo-Detroit-Chicago run, slips beneath an abandoned coaling tower on Conrail's former Michigan Central main line near Augusta, Michigan, in February 1989. Canon F-1, 50 mm, Fujichrome 50, 1/250th, f6.7

One of the most enjoyable aspects of railroad photography is capturing a train in its environment, sometimes dwarfed by the magnificent scenery. The resulting images are often part railroad, part landscape, which I like to call "trainscapes." Whether you'll be shooting trains in New Jersey or Nevada, look for areas that lend themselves to making trainscapes.

On March 16, 1991, Denver Rio Grande & Western's ROGJM (Roper yard, Salt Lake to Grand Junction, Colorado) nears Desert Siding west of Green River, Utah, on Subdivision Five.

Fuji GSW690II, 65 mm, Fujichrome Velvia 50, 1/250th, f6.7, tripod

New Jersey Meadowlands Area. Sandwiched between the urban backdrop of Hoboken and Union City, N.J., on the east and Harrison and Lyndhurst on the west lies a small, unremarked area of marshland along the Hackensack River that is probably home to more passenger trains than anywhere in the hemisphere. In an area little more than two miles long (looking north to south) are PATH, NJ Transit, Amtrak (Northeast Corridor), and Conrail crossings of the "Hack" river on six separate drawbridges. In the background can be seen the twin towers of the World Trade Center in Manhattan.

Obviously, the morning and evening rush hours are ideal times to see this multitude of trains at work. Alas, this is mosquito heaven, so try shooting in the early spring or late fall. Access is difficult but not impossible and just requires adequate preliminary scouting.

New Orleans, La. Here in the deep South is fertile territory for excellent rail photography. The combined activities of Amtrak, CSX, Illinois Central, Kansas City Southern, Norfolk Southern, Southern Pacific, and Union Pacific provide an abundance of photo opportunities throughout this sprawling area.

The massive Huey Long Bridge spanning the Mississippi River is shared by both trains and automobiles and is the centerpiece of railfanning interests. Also of note is the NS crossing of Lake Pontchartrain via a 5-3/4-mile-long wooden trestle northeast of the city. The best time to visit New Orleans is in spring or fall.

Powder River Basin Region, Wyo. In the northeastern corner of Wyoming lie the rich and abundant coal fields of the Powder River Basin. Three players — BN, CNW, and UP — annually haul millions of tons of coal carved from huge, modern,

Conrail's SEFR1, enroute from Selkirk, New York, to Framingham, Massachusetts, passes through a clearing east of Canaan, New York, with its load of tri-level autoracks.
FujiGW690II, 90 mm, Fujichrome Velvia 50, 1/500th, f4.5

open pit mines nestled in the rolling grasslands. Daily, dozens of trains continuously move to and from or in and about the main mining area located between Donkey Creek Junction (near Gillette) and Bill, Wyoming. The best photo opportunities are within the same area, but tenacious Crawford Hill in Nebraska and BN's operating hub at Alliance, Nebraska, are also must-see spots. Temperatures can be extremely hot in the summer and bitterly cold in the winter.

Sand Patch, Pa. Sand Patch grade in rugged southwestern Pennsylvania is the former Baltimore & Ohio's crossing of the Allegheny Mountains. Here, CSX continues the battle with the steep mountain grades, tunnels, and winding track, moving more than twenty-plus trains per day between Pittsburgh and Baltimore. Helpers are used regularly, and Amtrak's eastbound Capitol Limited rolls through in

the morning. Three manned, interlocking towers can be found on the eastern slope. To the south, just over the Maryland border in Cumberland, CSX operates a large hump yard and locomotive repair shops. Cumberland is also a crew change point and is large enough to offer a choice of motels and restaurants. Photographing on the Sand Patch grade is enjoyable all year round.

Sandpoint, Idaho. High in the Idaho Panhandle surrounded by Montana to the east, British Columbia to the north and Washington to the west, Sandpoint has all the required ingredients for the railroad photographer. These include exceptional scenery, a high concentration of trains, and diversity, with Amtrak, BN, Montana Rail Link, and Union Pacific all funneling through town. Nice accommodations in a small, resort setting make Sandpoint a good base of operations from which to visit the region year round.

Especially noteworthy are the MRL tracks along Lake Pend Orielle and BN's tracks over the lake on a long steel trestle.

Soldier Summit, Utah. Soldier Summit in central Utah is the single most formidable obstacle that the Denver & Rio Grande Western Railroad must contend with in the state. The combination of long, heavy trains, tunnels, countless curves, required helper operation, and two Amtrak trains daily makes this portion of the Denver-to-Salt Lake line a prime location to capture the essence of mountain railroading. The neighboring Utah Railway, plus Union Pacific coal trains, add to the congestion. It is easy to photograph one train at several different spots, and I would encourage you to work between Thistle and Price, some 50 miles apart. All the necessary amenities can be found in Price. Due to the elevation, prepare carefully if you are

With trench lights aglow, a pair of Canadian Pacific SD40-2s powers an eastbound train of empty grain hoppers along the banks of the Thompson River, ten kilometers west of Spences Bridge in British Columbia. Canon F-1,. 200 mm, Fujichrome 100, 1/500th, f4.5

planning a winter trek to Soldier Summit.

Somerset, Ky. Centrally located in the geographic middle of Norfolk Southern's Cincinnati-to-Chattanooga main line, Somerset and the region both north and south is commonly known to railroaders as the Rathole because of its many curves and tunnels. Over the years, most of the tunnels have been daylighted, resulting in very deep cuts. Several impressive bridges exist, but most notable is the massive Cumberland River Bridge at Burnside, Ky. Traffic on this line is heavy and includes RoadRailers running through during daylight hours. Spring, summer, and fall are the best times of the year to photograph the Rathole.

Tehachapi, Calif. The joint Southern Pacific and Santa Fe route over the Tehachapi Mountains in Southern California is considered by many railfans to be the granddaddy of railroad engineering. Situated between Bakersfield to the northwest and Mojave to the southeast, Tehachapi is one of the busiest mountain railroad regions in the nation, and much of it is single track. Stretched out some 35 miles with over a dozen tunnels, Tehachapi is accessible at numerous spots, including the fascinating Loop, where longer trains cross over (or under) themselves.

Late March or early April is the ideal time to visit the Tehachapi Mountains with their lush, green fields and wildflowers. Sometimes maintenance-of-way forces are busy repairing sections of track from midmorning to the afternoon. Train traffic is often stopped or limited during these times.

Toronto, Ontario. If you are looking to add some international flavor to your photography outings, take a trip to Toronto in eastern Canada. This contemporary city provides an exciting backdrop for the busy railway activities. Canadian National and Canadian Pacific handle all the freight, but the passenger operations really steal the show with Amtrak, Government of Ontario Transit (GO), Ontario Northland, and Via Rail vying for the spotlight. Especially interesting are the GO Transit and Via Rail locomotive and car servicing facilities adjacent to one another on the city's southeast side. Also worth seeing are the unique former Trans European Express train sets operated by Ontario Northland from Toronto to North Bay. Toronto is fun to visit all year round, though winters are cold and crisp.

Tucson-Willcox, Ariz. The Sunset Route is Southern Pacific's main east-west corridor linking California with points east all the way to New Orleans, Memphis, and Chicago. A particularly photographic portion of this line lies between Tucson and Willcox on the Tucson Division's Lordsburg Subdivision, especially in and around Vail, Mescal, Benson, Dragoon, Cochise, and Willcox. SP's double-stack container trains frequent these rails, and Amtrak runs an eastbound and westbound train on alternate days. Because of the enjoyable weather in the southwest, try exploring the Sunset Route during the winter months.

Taking photos trackside

The world of trains and railroad photography can become an all-consuming passion, providing hours of conversation and a lifetime of fond memories. But none of the talk or reminiscing can come close to the actual experiences we have trackside, creating interesting railroad images in our own styles.

Four key elements contribute to the overall impact of our photography: location, camera angle or vantage point, lens selection, and composition. Let's look at each element in detail.

Selecting a Location

Whether you prefer the hot-pursuit approach of chasing one train over dozens of miles, or you choose to wait patiently along the main line in one spot, the setting in which you shoot trains should be captivating in and of itself. Look for bridges, trestles, barns, trees, depots, sweeping curves, wild flowers, and other foreground and background features that help enhance the shot. On a larger scale — as when shooting the trainscape type of scene that I like so

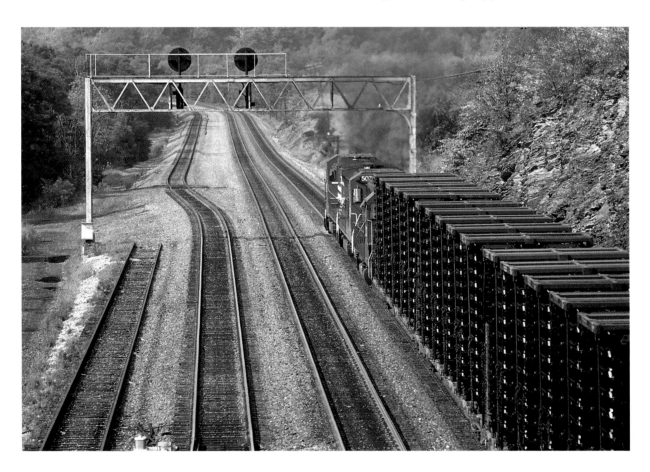

Often the train's consist will provide the variety that photos need. To achieve maximize results, avoid shooting the train head on or at ground level. Instead, look for hillsides or motor vehicle-pedestrian bridges that offer an unobstructed view of engines and freight.

(Opposite) Deep in the heart of Texas, near Pumpville, on SP's Sunset Route, AVMJU (Avondale, Louisiana, to Mojave, California) heads west with a unit train of water irrigation pipe. Canon T90, 300 mm, Fujichrome 50, 1/250th, f4.5

(Above) Making its way up the Allegheny mountains at CP Slope, just west of Altoona, Pennsylvania, Conrail's TV-11 carries a mixed load of auto frames on flat cars, along with piggyback trailers. Canon F-1, 400 mm, Fujichrome 100, 1/500th, f5.6

much — you'll want to include mountains and deserts, forests and lakes, and farms and fields in your compositions. Incorporating both trackside elements and the surrounding terrain helps to define the character of the railroad.

Finding a safe, attractive urban railroad setting can be considerably more challenging than finding a nice country spot, but with patience and a bit of exploration, it's possible. Look for yards or places where several lines intersect, and start from there. When you are in an unfamiliar city, stop at a hobby shop (one that sells model railroading products), and ask for directions to some interesting train watching spots nearby. If you live in the northern half of the United States or in Canada, you may want to do your city shooting during the winter months to take advantage of the clearer air or of a pristine covering of snow that often hides unattractive trackside debris. In any location, including a large expanse of sky can enhance your shots.

For future trips, make note of any interesting locales you find, even if you won't be returning for several months. Often, after a visit somewhere it becomes clear that train watching at that spot is better at certain times of the year or day; I try to remember that for upcoming trips.

Camera Angle

The camera angle you select and the vantage point you choose are just as important as finding the most interesting location. Before a train approaches, decide if you intend to emphasize the locomotives, the consist, or the entire train. During the first five or six months of my initiation to railroad photography, I shot the trains generally head on or from the

Using below-track-level shooting angles and wide-focal-length lenses make trains and locomotives appear more massive than they are. The low angle provides an additional benefit: the elimination of distracting background features.

(Left) Climbing the rugged mountain grade through Cajon Pass in Southern California, a Santa Fe SD45-2 in merger colors leads a short, eastbound freight near Summit. Canon T90, 24 mm, Fujichrome 50, 1/250th, f5.6

(Above) On a spring day in 1988, Missouri-Kansas-Texas (Katy) train No. 103 races across a small trestle near Sadler, Texas, on its southbound journey to Houston. Canon F-1, 20 mm, Fujichrome 100, 1/1000th, f-4

traditional 3/4-wedge viewpoint and all from about 6 feet above ground level. The shots I got of the engines were great, but I saw next to nothing of the train's consist or of the landscape. The large size of the locomotives (relative to the camera) blocked out the trailing train and background features. To solve this problem, I elevated the camera by shooting from an overlooking hillside or bridge. This perspective allowed me to get the desired frontal view of the engines while simultaneously being able to see the type of cars or loads on the train.

A low or below-track shooting angle makes the engines appear even more massive than they are, especially when shot with a normal or wide-angle lens. Additionally, a very low angle helps to eliminate a distracting background from the composition.

Broadside views are the best angles from which to photograph an entire train or to profile a certain locomotive. You don't, however, have to make all your shots from a 90-degree angle. The camera-to-track distance should be determined by three factors: how much of the train you want to see, how attractive the scenery is, and the focal length of the lens you are using.

Don't overlook going away shots either. They can be as dramatic and exciting as many approaching views — especially when you have the good fortune of photographing one train meeting another, perhaps on adjacent tracks, or when a slower freight is waiting in a siding. Additionally, going away shots really emphasize the type of train you are photographing — coal, double stack, military — as well as revealing a portion of the setting as seen from over and behind the lead units.

Lens Selection

Just as a skilled mechanic would carefully select the appropriate tool for the task at hand, the well-prepared railroad photographer needs to be adept at choosing the most suitable lens for a photograph.

One of the easiest and simplest ways to improve your photography is to avoid placing your subject in the center of the frame. Instead, use an off-center composition to create a more interesting balance. This technique works well with horizontal and vertical pictures.

(Above) Early in 1988, Pittsburgh and Lake Erie train MTPLE7 kicks up a fresh dusting of snow on Conrail's Southern Tier line near Smithboro, New York. The empty coal train is headed for home tracks after making a delivery to a New England generating station. Canon F-1, 400 mm, Fujichrome 100, 1/500th,f5.6

(Opposite page) Along the banks of the Thompson River near Spences Bridge, British Columbia, a pair of Canadian National 3600-horsepower SD50Fs makes light work of hauling a long string of empty grain hoppers east to the heartland. On the opposite side of the river lie the Canadian Pacific rails, momentarily quiet. Canon T90, 50 mm, Fujichrome 50, 1/250th, f5.6

Whether you own two lenses or ten, you can only use one lens per camera at a time. So it's important to size up each scene quickly and to determine what focal-length optic to use prior to the train's arrival.

I often think that my primary goal as a photographer is to extract the best possible image of the train or locomotive in each situation I encounter. The right lens in one setting may be completely inappropriate in the next. Essentially, the choice boils down to the amount of peripheral scenery I want to include in my train photo, be it a railroad yard, farm scene, landscape, or urban setting. The wrong lens may be too wide, including too many distracting features, or too tight, eliminating interesting aspects so that I don't see enough of the other "good stuff."

If you use multiple lenses, learn to alternate them frequently. This way you will produce a variety of different-looking images. Photos taken continually from the same perspective and with the same lens will look too similar, even if they consist of different scenes or types of trains. To break up the monotony, use a 28-mm or 50-mm lens for your morning shots and a 135-mm or 200-mm lens in the afternoon. The same goes for photographers using zooms — change the focal length from time to time. Also, don't be afraid to experiment or to use your lenses differently from the other photographers.

Composition

Beyond technical considerations, the final outcome of all our photographic efforts relies on the composition of each shot. Composition, according to the dictionary, is "the arrangement of elements in artistic form" and specifically means where we place the primary features in a photograph. A pleasing composition allows the train, a barn, the forest, and tracks to come together in a balanced and harmonious fashion. A poorly composed image includes the same features but in a busy, disjointed, or distracting way.

Regardless of the focal length of the lens you are

One way to make a routine photograph better is by framing the train so that your attention goes directly to it. The frame can be a window, a door frame, a pair of signals, or even a clearing between the leaves and branches of a tree.

(Above) In Cumberland, Maryland, Viaduct Tower operator Duane Boyd waves hello to the westbound crew of CSX engine 4290, rolling onto the Mountain Subdivision. You can almost feel the 102-degree heat and high humidity on this June 1988 day. Canon T90, 35 mm, Fujichrome 50, 1/250th, f5.6

(Opposite page) Just north of Hudson, New York, Amtrak No. 284, the *Niagara Rainbow*, banks into a curve enroute to New York City. Operating in the push-pull mode, the train is powered by two Rohr Turboliners, one operating at each end. Canon T90, 300-mm, Fujichrome 50, 1/500th, f4.5

One method used to create the illusion of motion in a still photograph is panning: using a slow shutter speed, a normal or wide-angle lens, and gently releasing the shutter while pivoting your upper body to track along at the same speed as your subject. The effects vary depending on the shutter speed and lens you use, as well as the subject's speed and the camera-to-subject distance.

(Above) A Southern Pacific locomotive appears to charge across the desert near Dragoon, Arizona, but is only going about 25-miles per hour. Canon F-1, 24 mm, Fujichrome 100, 1/8th, f6.7, approximately 20 feet away

Long exposures in the half second, one second, and multiple-second range offer an artistic alternative to the freeze frame world of conventional railroad photography. All you need is a sturdy tripod, a camera capable of making long exposures (most are), and a bit of experimental enthusiasm.

(Opposite top) At CSX's Cumberland, Maryland, shops an EMD unit still wearing its Chessie System colors gets a ride on the turntable before going back into active service. Canon T90, 24 mm, Fujichrome 50, 4 seconds, f6.7, tripod

(Opposite bottom) At 50 miles per hour, an eastbound Soo Line freight hustles toward Red Wing, Minnesota, on the former Milwaukee Road's Chicago-Twin Cities corridor. Canon F-1, 300 mm, Fujichrome 100, 1 second, f5.6, tripod

Stationary trains and locomotives can be photographed with a still camera and made to appear as though they are moving by using a technique called zooming. This is done by using a tripod-mounted camera equipped with a zoom lens (80-200-mm zooms are the most popular). Compose your shot at the maximum focal length. While making an exposure of a half second or longer, smoothly zoom the lens to its widest focal length setting. This produces a bursting effect, which looks quite dramatic.

(Left) Late on a Saturday afternoon in February, 1992, New Jersey Transit ALP44 No. 4402 sits at rest on a weekend layover in the sleepy bedroom community of Dover, New Jersey. Canon EOS-1, 80-200-mm zoom, Fujichrome Velvia 50, 2 seconds, f22, tripod

using, it is extremely important to keep your composition as simple and as graphic as possible. Doing so allows anyone who views your photographs to see the quintessence of each of your railroad scenes quickly and easily. If your wide-angle lens compositions include too much "garbage" (that can't be eliminated regardless of how you tilt and turn your camera or where you stand) switch to a longer lens such as a 50 mm, an 85 mm, or even a 135 mm. If that doesn't help, move to a better location.

There are many undesirable elements along the right-of-way that can often be cropped out by properly composing with the correct lens. These include: the photographer's shadow, shadows from telephone poles, the poles themselves, wires, buildings, adjacent roads and highways, tire tracks or footprints in the snow, and almost anything white — besides the train or snow. These distractions draw the eye away from the subject and weaken the impact of the shot.

Not only is it important to make visually clean shots of trains and rolling stock, but you should make images that are physically clean as well. That means taking the time to walk 30 or 40 yards to pick up a piece of trackside debris that appears in your frame. Otherwise, you may end up with a good-looking photo that's ruined by a piece of cardboard, a hunk of plywood, or section of strapping wire.

Two other elements of composition play a critical role in creating a dynamic image: the placement of the train or subject within the frame, and leaving "air" around your subject. Rather than allowing the lead units of a train to fall dead center in the middle of the frame when I make a photograph, I often use an off-center composition (which is inherently more interesting). For a horizontal shot, I keep the train near the upper or lower third of the frame with the balance of the shot being filled in with either an interesting foreground or a pretty sky. The first one or two engines are usually to the left or right of the viewfinder center. The same idea works well for vertical shots but in a slightly different manner. Imagine that your camera's viewfinder has a cross-hair focusing screen (they're available for many makes and models of cameras). You never want the largest or the most important portion of your subject — be it a person, locomotive, or the lead units of a train — to fall directly in the center of the crosshair. Many photographers call this the rule of thirds, and I highly recommend it for many of the shooting situations you encounter. Regardless of which part of the frame in which you like to place your train or engine, it's always essential to leave open a small section of track in front of your subject. That way, a person viewing your photograph knows that the train or engine has somewhere to go.

Additional Ways to Add Variety to Your Images

There are several simple ways to create railroad images that have a different look from previous train photos you made. One is to borrow a method that film makers have been using for years: varying the shooting distance from a long shot to a medium-distance shot to a close shot and then to an extreme close-up. Also, detail shots of heralds and emblems, gauges, and equipment add another facet to shooting static equipment. They make excellent transition images that can be used to help fill out a slide show or dress up a magazine page. Remember to make a few shots of the rail car loads, too. Coal, lumber, ore, army tanks, trucks, and autos are all part of the railroad's story.

Another way to make an interesting photo is to frame your subject by using some railroad or trackside element, such as a tree branch, siding sign, tunnel portal, or a window in a structure. Finding the right components that make a shot like this work is the hardest part of the job, but with patience and a watchful eye they'll come together for you.

A different approach is to allow the train or engine to take on a secondary role to a trackside element — either a natural or man-made one. No rule says the whole train must be seen all the time. I even think it's fine to let the train or engine go out of focus, as long as the result is a creative or unusual shot.

Additionally, take advantage of the out-of-focus foregrounds and backgrounds that occur when you shoot with long lenses. They help convey the feeling of depth or three-dimensionality.

Photographing Railroad People

Don't overlook the men and women who supervise, operate, and maintain the trains and physical plant of the railroads. Possibilities abound in all types of situations, but the best opportunities occur when crews are boarding and unboarding trains outside of yard limits. Another common situation is when a train must pull into a siding to let one or more higher-priority trains through, and a couple of crew members hop off to give a roll-by inspection.

One people situation I like to shoot particularly occurs when maintenance-of-way (MOW) forces are repairing or replacing a section of track. If the workers seem friendly or I have permission to be on railroad property, then I get in close (if it is safe) and shoot with my wide, normal, and short telephoto lenses to capture the action. I always ask the MOW. workers politely if they would mind putting on their hard hats and safety glasses for the four or five minutes I will be shooting. That way no one gets in trouble should the photo be published. If the people seem very friendly, I ask them if they would mind posing for an informal portrait. Then I get their names and addresses so I can send them a complimentary print or two later. Remember, these folks can provide some valuable information about their railroad, so courtesy goes a long way.

Sometimes you may not be able to get in as close to the railroaders as you might like, so using telephoto

Climbing up and out of Tunnel No. 10 in the Tehachapi Mountains of California, a long Santa Fe trailer train slithers along on joint SF/SP track prior to sunrise on April 11, 1989. Canon T90, 85 mm, Fujichrome 50, 30 seconds, f8, tripod

At Santa Fe's Barstow, California, yard, engine 5984, a 3600-horsepower EMD SDF45, idles on the service track. In the background, a trailer train moves out on the main. One of 40 such units built for the ATSF in 1982-83, No. 5984 has avoided the welder's torch and the painter's spray gun. Several SDF45s now see service in the Warbonnet livery, but this unit still roams the rails in the more conservative blue-and-yellow paint scheme. Fuji GSW690II Professional, 65-mm, Fujichrome 50, 1/125th, f9.5

Probably one of the fundamental ways to make a good shot great is to keep your compositions as simple and graphic as possible. Just as you select your location and lens prior to making each photo, you must determine what elements should be included or excluded in your final picture. At all costs, avoid distracting shadows, telephone poles, wires, cars, and highways unless those features play an integral part in your photograph.

(Left) Burlington Northern's High Line links the Pacific Northwest with the midwestern states. At Ethridge in northern Montana, a westbound grain train stretches out on the open, undulating plains. Canon F-1, 400 mm, Fujichrome 100, 1/500th, f6.7

(Below) On a warm September day in 1988, an Illinois Central southbound freight, pulled by a trio of SD20s and an SW14, motors along in the afternoon sun near Monee, Illinois. Canon F-1, 300 mm, Fujichrome 100, 1/500th, f5.6

Some 50 or so years ago, a train enthusiast thought to photograph the train he was chasing from a moving automobile, thus giving birth to the pacing shot. The techniques haven't changed. Find an open country road that parallels the tracks for a mile or two, get a driver for your chase vehicle, wait for a train to come along, and then pursue your train at the same speed it is traveling, shooting with 1/30th-, 1/15th-, 1/8th-, or 1/4th-of-a-second shutter speeds. The ideal pacing shots should be free of foreground fences, poles, and wires.

In April of 1989 on the Seligman Subdivision in Arizona, eastbound Santa Fe freight No. 804 cruises along behind a C30-7, GP39-2, GP60, and a B36-7. Fuji GSW690II Professional, 65 mm, Fujichrome 100, 1/30th, f32.

lenses in the 200-mm, 300-mm, and 400-mm range may be the only way to get good shots.

Creating the Illusion of Motion in Still Photos

Railfan photographers routinely work with fast shutter speeds such as 1/1000th, 1/500th, and 1/250th of a second to freeze the movement of a passing train. It's nice, however, from time to time to break from that traditional style of railroad photography. The use of slow shutter speeds opens up an entirely new world to the shooter who wants to create dynamic images that convey the feeling of speed and motion. There are four main ways to accomplish this, and all four require that you work with slower ISO films and shutter speeds in the range of 1/30th of a second and longer.

Panning. The first method — and probably the easiest to perfect — is called panning. After setting your shutter speed at 1/30th, 1/15th, or 1/8th of a second, meter normally and set the lens to the appropriate aperture. Then, as fluidly as possible, pivot your upper body in a small arc following along with the lead units of your train, releasing your shutter as gently as you can to prevent vertical shake. When properly executed, the resulting image will have a streaked background and foreground, while the locomotives will be mostly sharp. Several variables affect the final outcome: the train's speed, camera to subject distance, shutter speed, and focal length of your lens. Most often, I use lenses in the 35-mm to 85-mm focal length for panning. Practice makes perfect, so try shooting some buses or trucks on a nearby roadway until you get the hang of it.

Pacing. Pacing is somewhat similar to panning, but it requires that the photographer shoot from a moving vehicle traveling parallel to the train at or near the same speed. While directing the driver of the chase vehicle to slow down or speed up, the photographer uses slow shutter speeds in the range of 1/30th to 1/15th of a second. When done correctly, the entire set of locomotives or the train is totally sharp with the foreground rushing past in a blur. The ideal pacing shots are free of distracting fences and telephone lines. Use the same length lenses that you employ for panning shots.

Long exposures. Another altogether different way to communicate the excitement of movement in a still photograph is to mount your camera on a tripod, use a long shutter speed (anywhere from 1/30th of a second to 30 seconds) and make your exposures as your train or engine moves through your composition. This technique is most effective and easiest to execute at dawn or dusk, when illuminated locomotive headlights and trackside signals provide vivid color and stand out prominently from the background. The final results vary, from recognizable blurs to ghostly trails of trains, depending upon the length of your exposure and the speed of the train. Though experimental, these time exposures can be a

Kicking up a dust storm in its wake, a heavy-tonnage eastbound Southern Pacific freight reaches the first section of single track iron at Bena, California, on its climb up the Tehachapi Mountains. Canon F-1, 400 mm, Fujichrome 100, 1/500th, f5.6

pleasing alternative to the conventional photo of a train captured at 1/500th of a second.

Zooming. One other technique that can be utilized to convey a sense of motion, even with a stationary object, is called zooming. It is performed with a zoom-lens-equipped camera mounted on a tripod. First set your shutter speed for a 1- or 2-second exposure. Then take a light reading, adjust your aperture accordingly, and compose and focus with the focal length of the lens at its maximum (longest) setting. While simultaneously making your exposure, zoom the lens out to its widest focal length. This produces a bursting effect that is spectacular and enhances many static equipment shots. Head-on vertical shots work especially well, but try a few zooms using a horizontal composition.

Dozens of retired Duluth, Missabe & Iron Range cabooses stand at parade rest on a winter day at the railroad's Proctor, Minnesota, yard. Canon T90, 135 mm, Fujichrome 50, 1/125th, f5.6

Special situations

Taking daytime trackside photographs of trains and the activity immediately around them represents only one dimension of railroad photography. To add richness and diversity to your collection of train photography you should consider broadening your efforts; this chapter will help you do that.

Shooting from the Air

The use of small, fixed-wing aircraft and helicopters presents numerous benefits to railroad photographers who usually confine themselves to landborne photography. These include location scouting, unique perspectives, and most importantly, the ability to photograph multiple trains over dozens of miles of changing scenery.

Small planes and competent pilots can be found at hundreds of airfields dotting the United States and Canada. Rates range from $50 to $75 per hour for a two- or four-seat plane. This price includes the pilot's fee. Whenever possible, look for an aviation service that uses high-wing airplanes, since the low-wing design planes don't allow enough unobstructed downward visibility. Also, it's essential that aircraft you consider chartering — whether a plane or helicopter — be equipped with a window that opens so you can photograph without the glare and distortion encountered when shooting through plexiglass. The larger the opening, the better.

Obviously, the main advantage of using a small plane is the reasonable hourly rate and availability factor. The main disadvantage is that you are required to maintain an altitude of 500 feet in rural areas or 1,000 feet in populated areas. Flight may also be restricted in control zones due to other air traffic. Another disadvantage of using planes is that you seldom are able to fly along at the same speed as your train. Therefore you have to circle your prey continuously and waste time. However, planes do offer a lot for the money invested.

Helicopters are the ultimate shooting platform and can stay right with the train at virtually any speed and altitude (in rural areas or over water). During the six or seven times that I've employed jet helicopters for aerial assignments, I've made use of their other unique flight capabilities as well: hovering from 10 feet and up, flying backwards or sideways while pacing a train, and landing in fields or on clear mountaintops to wait for other railroad action, thus saving expensive rotor time. The downsides of using a helicopter are that they are much more expensive to charter per hour than planes, and they are seldom available where you want them. This is because of the high cost of operation and maintenance. The smaller and slower reciprocating helicopters (such as the Bell 47, the Enstrom F-28A, the Hughes 300, and The Robinson R-22) carry either one or two passengers (depending on model) and range from $150 to $200 per hour, including pilot. The larger and faster turbine helicopters (such as the Bell Jet Ranger or the Aerospatiale A-Star) can carry four passengers and range from $400 to $800 per hour, including pilot. Of the two helicopters, the Jet Ranger is more widely available with a national average hourly rate of approximately $500 per hour. (That's $8.33 per minute!)

Two ways to make an airborne adventure affordable are to get a local realtor or business person who needs aerials of property or facilities to foot the bill for all or a portion of the time, or to share the expenses by bringing some friends along, perhaps some that have never flown before. The $500 expense for an hour of Jet Ranger time divided among four passengers is only $125 each, surely manageable for a once-in-a-lifetime experience.

Incidentally, the best way to find helicopter services in your state is to look through the yellow pages under Aircraft Charter, Rental & Leasing. If none is listed, contact one of the larger general aviation companies and ask for a referral.

With the exception of a haze filter, used once in a great while, there is no special equipment required for air-to-ground shooting. To get optimal results, however, fly only on the clearest of days, either early

---

To make a correct exposure of a sunrise or sunset, virtually never include the actual ball of sun in your frame or metering pattern when measuring light. Otherwise, the intensity of the sun will cause you to stop down three, four or even five f-stops — resulting in a very dark photograph. Instead, point your camera toward the sky to the left, right, or above the sun and meter normally, then compose and shoot.

A cool October sunrise at Donkey Creek, Wyoming, finds an eastbound, loaded Burlington Northern coal train passing a train of empties. These tracks seldom remain quiet for long as Donkey Creek sits on the north end of a new (1979) 127-mile line to the Powder River Basin mines. The mines produce 600-million pounds of coal per day. Canon F-1, 300 mm, Fujichrome 100, 1/500th, f4

in the morning or later in the afternoon. I use the 24-, 35-, 50-, and 85-mm lenses for helicopter work and recommend optics in the 50-, 85-, 135-, and 200-mm focal length for the higher flying airplanes. Generally, my film of choice is Fujichrome Velvia Professional pushed to ISO 100 for the extra contrast (which helps to cut through haze) and speed. Just remember to select the fastest shutter speed possible — 1/250th, 1/350th, or 1/500th of a second are ideal. Don't brace yourself or your camera against the door or window of the aircraft. This maximizes vibration and camera shake. Instead, allow the natural shock absorption of your upper body and arms to aid in stabilization.

Don't forget to bring along a scanner with ear plugs to monitor train movements and a notebook or topographical map for jotting down future shooting locations that you may discover. Though you may be able to afford an aerial photo flight only once every few years or even once in your lifetime, it could prove to be one of the most exhilarating trainchasing experiences that you'll ever have.

Lighting Equipment for Interiors and Nighttime Rail Scenes

There are two schools of thought among photographers who shoot railroad facility interiors and the nocturnal rail scene. One approach is to work with the natural available light illuminating the subject. Another is to use artificial lighting to either supplement the available light or to illuminate the entire setting artificially. Both methods are effective and are discussed in the next two segments. An overview of some of the lighting equipment, predominantly electronic flash outfits (also called strobes), are mentioned here as a primer. As a standard of reference, I've included the approximate light output (measured in watt seconds) of each electronic unit listed. The higher the watt second number, the greater the intensity of the flash. This corresponds to an increase in price.

Low and Medium Powered Portable Flash Units

The small battery operated flash units in this category are the most popular choice of many photographers because of their modest size, light weight, automatic operation, and economical cost. Several camera manufacturers offer dedicated strobes tailor-made for their own lines of cameras. This type guarantees a perfect exposure in most situations and makes outdoor fill-flash shots simple. The best models allow you to use the flash in the manual mode as well. Most of the strobes made by camera manufacturers are in the 40- to 80-watt second range.

The best choices among the low-power non-camera manufacturer flash units are the Vivitar 283 and 285 HV. They're both inexpensive, rated at 60 watt seconds, and feature manual and automatic (though not dedicated) operation.

Incidentally, automatic flash units have a built-in electronic eye that senses how much light is bouncing off your subject; dedicated units operate in a more sophisticated, and accurate, manner and measure the

If you're looking for a fresh perspective on your regular shooting locations or if you want to follow one or more trains over dozens of miles, consider aerial photography. Though extremely expensive, helicopters are the best camera platforms, capable of sophisticated maneuvering, including hovering, backwards, sideways, and low level flight. In remote areas, it's even possible to set the helicopter down and wait for the next train to come along.

(Above) On March 12, 1991, an 8-unit lash-up carefully guides Union Pacific's NPLAF down the 2.2 percent gradient of Cima Hill in the high desert of southeastern California. One of the steepest grades on the railroad, Cima is located 81 miles from Las Vegas. Canon EOS-1, 50 mm, Fujichrome 50, 1/500th, f4.5

(Opposite bottom) Westbound TV-201, one of Conrail's highest priority intermodal trains, rolls along at 50-miles per hour behind a pair of GE C40-8Ws on the Chicago Line near Oneida, New York. The going will be good for only a few more minutes on this spectacular fall day in 1991. The engineer of 201 will have to take the siding to allow a faster TV-261 to overtake him and an eastbound Amtrak to pass. Canon F-1, 24 mm, Fujichrome Velvia 50 pushed to ISO 100, 1/500th, f5.6

The same train as on page 99, Conrail's Westbound TV-201, but this time photographed from behind the locomotive. Helicopters allow you to get photographs of the same train from many different positions and angles.

light coming back from your subject through the lens, telling both the flash and camera how to adjust. The larger, medium-powered "potato masher" flash units provide at least double the power of the smaller units. The Metz 45 CT/CL series of strobes are 145 watt seconds and their bigger counterparts, the 60 CT series, are rated at 160 watt seconds.

Another flash, the Sunpack Super 622, also has a watt second rating of 160. Both of these feature manual and automatic modes. Additionally, they can be made to function as dedicated units by purchasing and plugging in the appropriate module and cord for your camera.

A wide assortment of accessories is available for the above strobes. Of primary importance are the after-market rechargeable battery packs such as those made by Quantum. They allow for much faster recycling and provide more flashes per charge than either alkaline or nicad batteries. Quantum has five models of batteries and dozens of connecting cords and power modules from which to choose. These, in turn, interface with your specific model flash.

Also of interest are the light-modifying reflectors and domes used to soften and redirect the harsh flash illumination. These products are available from both the flash manufacturers and after-market companies like Lumiquest and Sto-fen. The good news about these products is that they're very inexpensive. The bad news is that you may lose one to three f-stops worth of light, depending on the modifier and how it is used. This forces you to work closer to your subject or at a larger aperture than you may like.

If you're looking into purchasing a new flash setup and are considering any night shooting, I strongly recommend that you bite the expense bullet and purchase either the Metz or Sunpack units. (Prices range from $200 to $600 depending on the model.) Though they are borderline regarding night shooting requirements, they do offer plenty of punch in most other situations and will give you years of dependable service.

High-Powered Portable Flash Units

At certain times, you may find that you need more light than is available from small and mid-sized flash equipment. Fortunately, three companies provide portable high-powered strobe setups that can be purchased (or rented) from your camera dealer. All are heavy, expensive, and can be used only in the manual mode. The light output must be measured with a flash meter or calculated by using a guide number. The Lumedyne flash system is the smallest, most modular, and affordable. Prices start around $500 for 200-watt seconds. It features multiple options of power packs, batteries, flash heads, booster modules, and accessories. The basic outfit is either a 200-watt seconds or 400-watt seconds unit, but it can be customized to 2400-watt seconds at the cost of increased weight and additional expense by the user. This is done by simply stacking on the appropriate booster packs and using the higher output flash head.

Another popular, portable, high-powered flash outfit is the Norman 200C (200-watt seconds.) and its big counterpart, the 400B (400-watt seconds). Both

Small single-engine aircraft and pilots can be found at airfields all across the United States and Canada. They provide reasonably inexpensive flight service. Their drawbacks: altitude restrictions and the inability to follow constantly along with the train due to its higher speed. You can still get a lot for your money in a plane, so consider a photo flight on some spring, summer or fall day. Canon EOS-1, 50 mm, Fujichrome Velvia 50 pushed to ISO 100, 1/500th, f6.7

When large windows allow substantial light to illuminate an interior scene, use daylight film. Then handhold or mount your camera on a tripod and shoot with slower shutter speeds like 1/60th, 1/30th, or 1/15th of a second. Although the least complicated approach to photographing interiors, this method always results in the outdoor scene — if visible through a door or window — being over-exposed.

In CSX's West Hump Control Tower in Cumberland, Maryland, yardmaster Mike Stump talks with the head office while trying to sort out a blocking problem on June 20, 1988.

Canon F-1, 24 mm, Fujichrome 100, 1/60th, f5.6

are extremely durable units that are used by hundreds of news, sports, and location photographers worldwide. Though there are fewer options with the Norman strobes, they still provide the basic necessity you may crave: a lot of light from a shoulder-carried flash system. The 200-watt second unit costs $650, and the 400-watt second unit is $750.

Out of the box, the highest powered, most expensive self-contained flash unit is the Comet PMT-1200 (1,200-watt seconds). Weighing in at 12.15 pounds, this power pack, battery, and flash head outfit delivers forty-five walloping full-power blasts of light per battery charge. Recycling takes six to seven seconds. That's surely enough rapid fire power to make any nighttime rail photographer smile. However, the $2,800 price tag makes the PMT-1200 workable only if you are extremely wealthy, can use it all the time (and justify the expense), or can rent one from time to time for those special shooting sessions.

High-Powered Studio/Location Strobes

Studio/location flash equipment provides you with the most controllable, natural-looking lighting setup available. Numerous manufacturers offer one of two types of strobes: monolights which have a power pack and flash head built in to one self-contained unit, or separate flash heads connected to separate power packs (most of which have three or four head outlets each). Monolights are less expensive but are heavier and limited to 200-, 400-, or 600-watt seconds, depending on make and model. The a la carte type of strobes with separate components commonly can be found with power pack and head combinations that put out anywhere from 500- to 4800-maximum-watt seconds. The more affordable units, however, are in the 500-, 800-, 1000-, 2,000-, or 2,400-watt second range. All models of alternating current-powered strobes feature adjustable modeling lights that closely resemble the quality and direction of light of the flash. This gives you the opportunity to preview and evaluate lighting placement before shooting any film. Almost all models of studio/location strobes

accept a wide variety of accessories such as reflectors, barn doors, colored gels, and light-diffusing soft boxes or umbrellas. The separate head and power pack flash outfits are commonly the most available for rental and can usually be found for under $100 per day/weekend. An outfit consists of one of each of the following: head, power pack, light stand, umbrella, flash meter, and a polaroid-type camera for making proofs of your light setup. By renting an additional one or two flash heads, you can light a larger area and/or create a more evenly balanced lighting situation.

Look at Comet, Dyna-Lite, and Speedotron when selecting the separate flash head/power pack type of strobe equipment. Dyna-Lite units are my favorite because they are small, lightweight, and provide plenty of power for most situations. If you are renting monolights, check out models made by Bowens, Broncolor, Sunpack, and White Lightning.

Regardless of what equipment you own, use a sand bag or weight to stabilize any lights on stands. Several long extension cords are also handy to have when using AC strobe equipment. Real remote shooting can be performed with up to 2,000-watt seconds' worth of AC strobes if you borrow or rent a voltage-regulated generator such as those made by Honda, Kawasaki, Nissan, and Yamaha. Triggering devices called slaves can be plugged into each of your power packs or monolights so that multiple units can be fired simultaneously. In good weather, this could provide a viable alternative to lighting large night scenes. For in-depth information about slaves and generators, flash equipment (large or small), and many other aspects of artificial lighting, I highly recommend *Adventures in Location Lighting*, 5th Edition, John Falk ($29.95.) It is published in cooperation with Eastman Kodak and is packed with tech tips and lighting wizardry know-how.

Photo Flashbulbs

Years ago, before the development and widespread use of electronic flash equipment, photographers relied entirely upon flashbulbs to make both interior

When an enclosed interior scene is predominantly lit by Tungsten lights (the incandescent type in your home), use Tungsten film balanced for that light source.

(Top) At Alliance, Nebraska, dispatcher Jerry B. Johnson pencils in another coal train movement on Burlington Northern's Orin Line in Wyoming. Canon T90, 24 mm, Fujichrome 50 Tungsten, 1/15, f2.8, tripod

The green cast given off by flourescent lights is troublesome for daylight films. Ultimately, you have two options: shoot the scene as is and live with it or use a 30 or 40 cc magenta color-correction filter, which will help a little.

(Bottom) John Hein, terminal car movement clerk with the C & NW at Proviso yard's camera room, is recording ID numbers on incoming freight cars. I shot without filters because I didn't want the TV monitors to appear magenta. Canon T90, 35 mm, Fujichrome 50, 1/4th, f5.6, tripod

and exterior photographs inexpensively. Though considered a dying art, many railroad photographers still use flashbulbs (also called photoflash lamps) to light very large twilight and nighttime rail scenes with a minimal amount of equipment.

The most commonly used type of flashbulbs are GE No. 22s and Sylvania No. 2s — both types are available as surplus only — and the PF-200 bulbs currently produced by EG&G Electro Optics. When available, the surplus bulbs sell for $2.50 to $3 each, while new fresh bulbs go for $6 each. All are balanced for use with Tungsten film, but many photographers use them with daylight film for a warmer look.

Though the light output of flashbulbs is calculated differently than that of electronic flash, the bulbs sizes mentioned deliver the equivalent of about 1,200 watt seconds. Two surplus variants, the 22B and 2B, have a blue coating that makes them balanced for use with daylight film but cuts their output by one f-stop.

Flashbulbs are usually fired by a handheld, battery-powered flash gun with built-in reflector, but multiple guns can be wired together and tripped with a high-voltage battery.

Since many typical night scenes require three, four, or even five bulbs per shot, the high cost of using flashbulbs becomes apparent quickly. It's not out of the ordinary for a couple of photographers working jointly on a nocturnal shoot to spend $50 to $60 on bulbs.

If you do that once a month for a year, you will spend enough to buy a new Lumedyne or Norman electronic flash setup. It wouldn't be quite as powerful, however, as the No. 2 type bulbs. If you spend a bit more money, the Lumedyne can be configured to provide equivalent power.

Some critics argue that the quality of light from a flashbulb is superior to the light of an electronic flash unit. They feel that flashbulbs create better color saturation and a more natural color rendition. I feel, however, that strobes can light any subject as well as flashbulbs. Yes, the initial expense of strobes is substantial, and some exposure testing and filtration may be required, but the extra control, repeatability, rapid recycling, and relatively large battery capacities of electronic flash equipment outshine the usefulness of flashbulbs. Ultimately, you have to choose what way to go. Nevertheless, I recommend *The Railroad Night Scene* by Preston Cook and Jim Boyd (Old Line Graphics, 128 pages, $44). It's loaded with great photos, all lit with flashbulbs, and serves as an in-depth guide to night-lighting theory and practice. This is a top-quality book that you should read, even if you'll never consider using flashbulbs.

Photographing Inside Railroad Buildings

From time to time you may have the opportunity to visit a dispatching center, interlocking tower, locomotive shop, or other rail-related facility to make photographs. Once inside, determine the dominant type of light illuminating your interior scene: daylight, tungsten, fluorescent, or some other source (such as sodium vapor or mercury vapor). The second thing to consider is how to best deal with the situation at hand. This is directly affected by your

time, access, and interest in getting the perfect shot. Listed here are several lighting scenarios and the options you can employ to handle them.

Available Light / Daylight Illumination
Location: Yard tower with lots of windows and overhead fluorescent lights

Start by asking the yard master if you can shut off the flourescents. If left on, they could contaminate your shot with a green cast. Then, open all blinds or shades so that the maximum amount of daylight streams in. For additional speed, shoot with ISO 100 film with your fastest normal or wide-angle lens. Depending on the scene's relative brightness, steadily shoot your handheld camera at 1/30th- or 1/15th-of-a-second shutter speeds. If longer exposures are necessary, use a tripod along with a cable release, and ask your subject to be as motionless as possible. Be aware that the outside scenes in your composition will be washed out. This is due to the three, four, or five f-stop difference between inside and outside light levels.

Available Light / Tungsten Illumination
Location: Dispatcher's office with no windows

Tungsten light sources are any incandescent bulbs that give off illumination within a certain band or spectrum of color (different from the color of daylight). This includes regular household bulbs. The photographer has the choice of using a color correcting filter on the lens so that the tungsten is balanced for daylight film or simply shooting the scene with tungsten film, which is specifically designed for exposure under tungsten illumination. (If you should accidentally shoot daylight film in tungsten light, your subjects will have an unappealing orange cast.)

The second option is better because you don't have to buy special filters or worry about light loss due to the filter's density. As in the first scenario, use your camera mounted on a tripod and gently squeeze your shots off while the dispatcher is as still as possible. Since light levels will be much lower than those in the first scenario, expect some motion or blurring of your subject. Also, if any video screens are included in your composition, use a shutter speed of 1/15th of a second or slower to avoid bands appearing on the televised image. Then, process Tungsten film normally.

Available Light / Fluorescent Illumination
Location: Dispatcher's office with no windows

If it is necessary to photograph with available light in a fluorescent-lit room, the only options you have are to use color correction filters on the lens with daylight film in the camera or live with a green slide. The FL series of filters adds thirty to forty units (varies by filter manufacturer) of magenta filtration to compensate for the obnoxious green cast emitted by fluorescent lights. Proceed with your shooting as in the second scenario. In my opinion, however, working in fluorescent light is undesirable. Usually,

Though AC-powered location-studio strobes are heavy and cumbersome, they provide natural looking light inside small- to medium-interior spaces, and they put out enough raw light to balance the inside exposure with the outside.

(Top) At Conrail's MO Tower in Cresson, Pennsylvania, operator Jay Bimle watches a train come on the circuit while outside a set of helpers head east to Altoona for another assignment. Canon T90, 28 mm, Fujichrome 50, 1/250th, f6.7, one Dynalight 800-watt second power pack with two flashheads

---

An alternative to the minimalist available-light method of photographing interior scenes is to use an electronic flash. If you are using a small- to medium-power flash unit there can be a rapid fall off of light and hot spots.

(Bottom) At the Burlington Northern dispatcher's office in Alliance, Nebraska, relief chief dispatcher Bill DeLett checks the disposition of locomotive assignments on the board. Canon T90, 35 mm, Fujichrome 50, 1/125th, f5.6, Metz 45CT-4 flash

By far the easiest approach to making nighttime photographs is to work with available light. No fancy equipment is required, just a creative eye, some experimenting, time, and a tripod.

On the south side of Union Pacific's Bailey yard in North Platte, Nebraska, a set of SD40-2s idle on the hump while a long string of cars are marshaled past on October 2, 1988. An afternoon rainstorm has left a pool of water in a normally dry lot, providing the mirror reflection of sky and equipment. Canon T90, 35 mm, Fujichrome 50, 8 seconds, f11, tripod

the results are disappointing because of inconsistencies between tube manufacturers and mixtures of brands and types.

Artificial Light / Low and Medium Powered Flash Illumination
Location: Dimly lit Dispatcher's office with no outside windows

With smaller, portable flash units, the best approach often lies in balancing the flash output with indoor illumination. Start by taking a regular light reading of the interior scene with your camera's built-in meter. With older cameras, you'll need to use a shutter speed of 1/60th of a second or slower to synchronize with the flash properly. Though newer, more sophisticated cameras can synchronize with a flash at shutter speeds all the way up to 1/250th of a

measure the light as accurately as possible. Any or all of these steps make a flash shot better and help the scene look more naturally illuminated compared to the typical on-camera, direct-flash approach.

Artificial Light / High Powered Flash Illumination
Location: Interlocking tower with lots of windows

Using an AC-powered flash outfit is more troublesome than the approaches used in other scenarios presented here, but the results are second to none. Here's how to use a rented Dynalite 800-watt second power pack and two flash heads. (Setting up a monolight outfit is virtually the same except for the lack of a separate power pack.) First, select a camera position and place your camera bag and power pack on the floor nearby. Place one flash head on a light stand and attach a large umbrella to diffuse and control the light of the strobe. Set it just to the left or right of your shooting position, with the flash head/umbrella 5 to 6 feet high (for a standing subject) and tilted slightly downward and directed toward your subject. This is your main light.

Next, place a flash head — minus the umbrella — on a light stand and aim it straight up at the white ceiling. Place this light as far into the room as possible but out of sight of the camera position. This is the fill light that indirectly illuminates the background area and softens many of the shadows made by the main light. Now, plug the power pack into the nearest outlet. Plug the camera-to-flash sync cord into the power pack as well. Then plug the two flash heads into the power pack, one head into bank A and the other into bank B. Next, turn on the built-in modeling lights; they closely resemble the look, but not the intensity, of the strobes. Reposition the lights or tilt the heads as necessary, being sure to watch for unwanted reflections. Turn off the modeling lights for a couple of minutes, then load a roll of Fujichrome 50 or other slow-speed film into your camera and walk over to the window. (If you are using a current model camera with fast flash sync speed (1/125th or 1/250th) you can balance the inside light with the exterior light of midday.

If you have an older model camera and want to balance the interior and exterior scene, you'll probably have to wait until dusk to allow the outside brightness to come down to a level that the strobes can match. Take a normal light reading of the outside scene through the glass. For example, if the meter tells you to use f5.6 at 1/250th, then f5.6 becomes the dominant number to which you'll match the flash output. Turn the modeling lights on again, and turn the flash power switch on. Set the rocker switch for your main light on bank A to 200-watt seconds. Then set the fill light on bank B to 200-watt seconds. Make sure the A:B ratio switch is set so that you can give either head more or less light as neccessary.

Now, take out the flash meter. Set it to 1/250th of a second — check the ISO, too — turn it on, and direct it toward the camera position while you are standing where the subject will be standing. Then ask a friend to hit the test fire button on the power pack and note the reading. If you need to change the

second, the low available light levels routinely encountered in situations like this will mandate a longer shutter speed. By the way, you'll probably want to use a medium-speed film such as ISO 100 to get the most out of the flash illumination.

Next, set your flash to the appropriate f-stop output setting, one that matches the aperture your meter recommends. Now, evaluate your scene, looking for problem areas such as extremely light walls or reflective surfaces that can both fool the flash into an incorrect exposure and cause a distracting glare. Then, shoot away.

Several factors can help you make better interior flash shots: an off camera flash; bouncing some or all of the light off the ceiling; using a flash reflector to modify the light; using multiple units to create a broad, evenly lit scene; and, perhaps, using the flash in the manual mode and using a flash meter to

light intensity, set the power on bank A at 100-watt seconds or 400-watt seconds as required. Repeat the metering process with the fill light on bank B, but this time take the reading at the back of the room. Adjust the power accordingly. Unless you are looking to achieve some dramatic effect, try to keep the levels of the two lights within a one-f-stop range of each other. A little bit more control can be had by moving the lights closer or farther away from your subject. When both lights are reasonably close to f5.6, plug the sync cord into the proofing camera that you rented with the flash outfit. Take a Polaroid and evaluate the scene, looking for distracting shadows, reflections, cords, and so on. When you are happy with the way the shot and lighting look, it's time to make real photos. Grab your main camera, plug in the sync cord, wait for a train to appear in the window, and then make a great shot of your tower operator at work.

Using studio strobes isn't hard or complex. It just requires a bit of practice and some familiarity with the equipment.

Photographing the Nighttime Railscene

For most railfans, the shooting day ends with the setting sun, but for a large number of enthusiasts dusk marks the arrival of another photographic challenge. The attractions are multifaceted, and each person has his own reasons for photgraphing at night. For some, it's the extended shooting time that's unhampered by work, school, or family commitments. Others find the sense of discovery, experimentation, and solitude enjoyable. Still others get satisfaction out of making different images while working with close friends.

The elements involved in executing a nocturnal shoot vary, starting with the degree of difficulty, which ranges from elementary to complex. The scale of scenes can also vary from close-ups of engines to massive yards, and the cost of involvement ranges from inexpensive to great. That's the beauty of nighttime photography. You can tailor your involvement and investment to suit your interests, goals, and budget. Listed here are examples of nighttime photography and the options you can employ to handle them.

Working with Available Light Only
Location: Railyard with substantiall overhead light illuminating subject.

By working exclusively with the ambient light at a shooting location, you are taking the easiest and least expensive approach to creating a nighttime photo. All that's required is a slow-speed film, a camera with a few prime lenses, a tripod, perhaps a cable release, and optionally, a flashlight to help you see the controls on your camera.

Just as you would for a daytime shot, mentally evaluate the interesting aspects of the scene, select a camera position, and choose the best lens accordingly. Next, load your camera, and mount it on your tripod. Before making the final composition, take a light reading off a fairly neutral gray surface, such as the

(Top) Available light for nighttime photography seldom yeilds slides that are 100-percent color accurate — because of the dramatic mismatch between your film and the light source illuminating the overall scene. You either have to accept the off-color cast — which isn't always so bad — or develop a variety of color-correction filter packs for each different light source you'll encounter. Canon F-1, 85 mm, Fujichrome Velvia 50 at 100, 8 seconds, f5.6, tripod

(Bottom) At the end of New Jersey Transit's 22.3-mile-long Gladstone Branch in Gladstone, four sets of M.U. Arrows weather a March snowstorm in 1992. Notice how two different types of color-balanced film alter the mood and impact. Canon T90, 85mm, Fujichrome Tungsten 64, 30 seconds, f11, tripod, automobile headlights sweeping the scene to create areas of highlight

ballast, if it is lit similarly to your locomotive or rolling stock. This is where the long exposure features of modern electronic cameras come in handy. Simply set the shutter speed at fifteen, twenty, or thirty seconds. You're in luck if you have an older camera that will only meter down to a one-second exposure but that has a B setting (used for time exposures). With the shutter speed set to one second, take a light reading. If the meter tells you to use f2.8 but you'd like to stop down for greater depth of field, then calculate the correct exposure. For example, two seconds would give you an f-stop of 4, four seconds at f5.6, eight seconds at f8, sixteen seconds at f11, and thirty-two seconds at f16. With this approximate exposure in mind, set your camera to B, and make the desired exposure.

Regardless of the age of your camera, always bracket your exposures to compensate for the difficulty in getting an accurate exposure. Bracketing also compensates for reciprocity failure, a factor that causes films to shift in color balance and makes them prone to underexposure at long shutter speeds. To be safe, bracket in 1/2-stop intervals 1-1/2 stops over and 1-1/2 stops under the recommended reading at least until you get the hang of things.

The results of your available light shots will vary greatly depending entirely upon the type of light sources intermixing in your scene. You may find it worthwhile to shoot both daylight and tungsten color-balanced films to see how they react under different light conditions and which satisfies your color preference.

Sometimes it's fun to take a flashlight and highlight small parts of a locomotive during your exposure. This works especially well on Scotchlite-type unit numbers and the railroad heralds found on some engines.

Also, try experimenting by sweeping the scene with the headlights of your car to add some accent to your photograph.

Using a High-Powered Portable Electronic Flash at the Night Rail Scene
Location: Railyard with substantial ambient light throughout

The most popular approach to nighttime photography with artificial light is a technique called

Often in larger rail yards you'll find your subject illuminated primarily by bright, overhead lights of the mercury vapor/sodium type. Since shutting them off is usually out of the question, supplement the ambient light by using either strobes or flashbulbs to light the areas that otherwise would be in shadow. This will result in an image with greater detail.

At Dover, the largest outlying terminal on the New Jersey Transit commuter system, No. 4403, a Swedish-built ALP-44, poses for a nightime portrait on April 14, 1992. Two or three of these 7,000-horsepower locomotives call Dover home, although the railroad owns 15 ALPs altogether, with five more units on order. Mamiya RZ-67, 110mm, Fujichrome Velvia 50, 30-seconds, f4.5, tripod, Comet PMT-1200 portable flash providing two 600-watt seconds flashes on the front of the locomotive and three 600-watt second flashes on the side

painting with light or open-flash photography. This is done by opening the shutter for several seconds and firing your flash repeatedly from several positions until the subject is adequately and evenly illuminated. (The method described here is, in theory, virtually the same approach flashbulb users employ.)

To start, set your equipment up as in the previous scenario. After you have your subject composed and in focus, measure off the positions from which you'll fire your flash. With powerful units like the Comet PMT-1200, the Lumedyne flash system, and the Norman 400 B, the distance should be approximately 30 feet. Mark the equidistant spots from the subject with a rock or stick at both the front of the locomotive and down its side. Make sure those spots are out of the line-of-sight from the camera position. Ideally, you want to be able to make multiple overlapping flashes to light the entire locomotive. Depending upon the size of the unit, one frontal pop of the flash and three or four pops along the side should provide sufficient coverage.

Next, you need to determine the proper exposure. With the Comet PMT-1200 set at 1,200-watt seconds, make a test flash with a flash meter or calculate the correct exposure from the guide number. Guide numbers are reference ratings of a flash unit's maximum output that are divided by the flash-to-subject distance (in feet) to come up with an approximate f-stop. Open up or stop down your aperture if you are using a film speed slower or faster than ISO 100. Use slow films for this on most occasions, however, because of their superior color, sharpness, and low sensitivity to ambient light.

Now it's time to make a photograph. With the camera loaded and the aperture set, open the shutter and go to flash position No. 1, the front of the locomotive, and with the flash held at arm's length above your head, make pop No. 1. (The arm's height assures that the light will be evenly distributed on the full front of the locomotive, including long-nosed units.) Rapidly walk past the front of the camera, through the scene, from position No. 1 to position No. 2. If you are quick and wear semi-dark clothes, no image of yourself will be recorded on the film.

At position No. 2 pop the flash towards the front

On numerous occasions the locomotive or rolling stock may be barely lit or shrouded completely in darkness. Therefore, you may need to use flashbulbs, portable electronic flash, or the larger AC-powered studio strobes to light nearly the entire scene. This will enable you to make photos of proper contrast and clean color with crisp details.

Since Dover, New Jersey, is at the end of electrification on the Boonton and Morristown Lines, New Jersey Transit uses several diesel locomotive-powered train sets to serve commuters from western extremities such as Lake Hopatcong and Netcong. Under a reciprocal agreement, NJT and Metro North contribute motive power and equipment for each other to operate on neighboring lines. That's why Metro North GP40FH-2 No. 4188 idles under the Dover catenary on a foggy Easter night in 1992. Mamiya RZ-67, 110 mm, Fujichrome 50, 30-seconds, f5.6, tripod, Comet PMT-1200 portable flash providing one 1200-watt second flash to the front of the locomotive and four 1200-watt second flashes down the side

Across a snow-covered prairie, Union Pacific's NPYR, a daily North Platte, Nebraska, to Yermo, California, freight, idles on a siding at Champlin, Utah, on March 15, 1991. Fuji GW690 II Professional, 90 mm, Fujichrome Velvia 50, 1/250th, f6.7

Other Ideas about Nighttime Photography

Two ways to make your night shooting sessions as productive as possible are to use multiple cameras and/or a camera with a polaroid back. Several cameras on tripods allow you to make more images of the same scene at different apertures, ensuring that at least one exposure will be correct. (Try a 1/2-f-stop difference with each camera.) Consider shooting black-and-white and color simultaneously, if that strikes your fancy. A camera like the Mamiya RZ-67 or RB-67 equipped with an interchangeable Polaroid back provides visual confirmation of exposure and lighting placement in sixty seconds. By switching backs, you can use either camera alongside your 35-mm camera with conventional roll film.

Also, if you can't borrow, rent, or purchase a high-powered portable electronic flash, take heart. Smaller flash units like the Metz and Sunpack models can be used in many situations with fairly good results. You'll need to work in closer to your subject and the length of your exposures may be considerably longer, but that's the price you must pay. Remember, as long as the camera's shutter is open, you can make as many pops of the flash as you like. Since you have the benefit of faster recycling with small- and medium-powered strobes, you can fire a dozen or more flashes during an exposure. As mentioned in this chapter, the after-market batteries offered by Quantum dramatically increase flash capacity and recycling times.

If you're working on a shoestring budget, you may want to use the flashbulb method of illumination occasionally. Use flashblubs in situations such as rainy nights when it's not advisable to use high-capacity electronic flash gear.

Also, large-scale scenes requiring numerous light positions may be best suited to flashbulbs because of the expense involved in gathering multiple flash guns compared to renting multiple strobe units. Many photographers minimize the expenses of night lighting even further by using extension cords and photo floodlights (which can be purchased either daylight or tungsten balanced), and paint with light in the truest sense.

Another way to get great nocturnal results is to use rented studio strobes on location with a generator. Though you can only use them in dry weather, and it's an additional hassle to rent and set them up, the raw power and two-to-three second recycling of the Dynalite 800- or 1,000-watt second strobe packs make them real contenders. Because of the rapid recycling you can dump a lot of light in a short period of time. That allows shorter exposure times, which means more control over available light and more natural-looking pictures. Besides, night-shooting sessions are often planned days, weeks, and even months in advance, so why not take advantage of AC-powered flash equipment?

Just as there are an infinite number of alternatives to the 3/4-wedge photo taken during daylight hours, there are ways to make your night shots creative as well. Try including buildings, signals, crossing gates, people, and other rail-related subjects in your compositions.

side of the engine. Whenever possible, try to angle the flash so that any reflection is directed or bounced away from the camera position.

Continue with pops No. 3, No. 4, and, if necessary, No. 5. Then return to the camera and close the shutter. Repeat the whole process, working at a slightly different aperture until you feel you've gotten the shot or your batteries are dead. Congratulations! You've successfully made a series of nighttime photos.

Editing your slides and getting published

Exercise the same care and consideration when editing your slides as you do when selecting cameras, lenses, and film. All too often, fine novice and advanced photographers include far too many mediocre images in their portfolios or slide presentations thereby appearing to be not so talented. Railroad photographers are especially afflicted by this disease, which weakens the impact of each individual image. Not only is editing important when you are arranging an informal slide show or organizing your slide collection, but it's also essential when submitting your train photos to railfan magazines.

Editing Equipment

The first requirement for editing is an area that is dry, clean, uncluttered, and that can be used semipermanently for slide review and storage. If available, a small, spare bedroom or shared space in a sewing room is perfect. You can even make do with a closet. When I was a photography student at the Rochester Institute of Technology, I used a 4-foot wide closet with bi-fold doors as my editing station. A sheet of 30" x 48" x 3/4" plywood, a couple of 2 x 4s, and a few shallow shelves served me well for several years.

The most essential piece of equipment is a light box, often called a light table or viewing box. It provides a flat, evenly illuminated working surface for reviewing and sorting slides. The light sources on the best models are balanced at 5,000 degrees Kelvin. Thus, your slides can be viewed without the colored cast often found in unbalanced units. A variety of manufacturers offer light boxes in numerous sizes and price ranges. The smaller, inexpensive, portable models sell for less than $150. The midsized to larger models sell for $200 to $300 and up. Your existing slide collection, as well as your future editing needs, should be considered before purchasing a light box. Light boxes can be purchased at better camera stores and from the Calumet and Light Impressions catalog.

Other essential editing tools include:
• A 4x or 8x viewing lupe (also spelled loupe) to view the image and to look at each individual slide critically to determine if it is in focus.
• Dust-Off or another environmentally safe type of compressed air for cleaning slides.

• A trash can for discarding the bad shots.
• Clear-topped slide boxes for easy slide sorting, available from processing labs
• Adhesive labels for identifying your slide boxes and sorting trays.
• Magic markers and pens for marking labels and writing captions.
• Finally, as optional equipment, a stereo can add much enjoyment to a long editing session.

Keeping Track of What You Shoot

One important habit you should get into early in your trainchasing/phototaking career is logging information about each train you photograph. After trying to use bits of paper and small notebooks, I developed a simple and thorough railroad log on my computer. (A blank version appears at the back of this book. Feel free to adapt or reproduce it for your personal use.) A local print shop made up a few dozen 6-1/2" x 6-1/2" fifty-sheet pads for me, and I now use them for jotting down data for all the trains I shoot.

The key to identifying a photo of a certain train successfully is in the locomotive's lead number. That number appears near the top of the corresponding railroad log sheet. Get as much information about each train as possible, from a train crew, track inspector, or other railway worker, and by closely monitoring your scanner.

When I'm working in an extremely busy location, I often use an inexpensive voice activated tape recorder — stuffed into my shirt pocket — to record the engine number, direction of travel, train symbol, and other pertinent information for each passing freight. Then, when the action dies down, I transfer the information to the log sheets.

At home, I keep the sheets separated by road name and stored in manila envelopes. When searching for certain caption information, inevitably I find that I've photographed the same lead engine on several different occasions, possibly in the same area. This is where accurately recording the consist, weather, camera, lens, film, and other remarks can help distinguish one image from the next. As an example, make note of whether the shot is horizontal or vertical, wide angle or telephoto, and if the train is coming downgrade or smoking uphill. Taking a

---

A Canadian National grain and sulphur train snakes through an S-curve in the Thompson River Canyon at Martel siding in British Columbia. Canon F-1, 200 mm, Fujichrome 100, 1/500th, f5.6

Detail photographs add texture to your railroad photo collection. Be sure to take a few whenever there is a lull in the action. Clockwise from opposite top left: "K" Line logo on an intermodal container, headlight and air horn on a Santa Fe C30-7, Canadian National Maple Leaf logo on a boxcar, fuel cap on a scrap heap bound Conrail locomotive, freshly painted brake wheels on C&NW flat cars, a front marker plate on a Burlington Northern SD40, a rusty pile of rail spikes awaiting recycling, and a newly painted herald on a C&NW covered hopper.

minute or two to fill out a log sheet will make captioning your photos a breeze, months or even years later.

Developing an Intelligent Approach to Editing

Develop an efficient and systematic approach to editing before doing anything else. Think of all the categories your photos fall into and how to organize them best. A little forethought now can save lots of effort later. Plus, it takes the drudgery out of the task. After one of my earlier and longer photo expeditions, I found myself confronting some ninety rolls of film to review, sort, and edit. I didn't know how to even begin. So, I simply put the project aside for more than a month. Not until I thought through the required final categories could I start (and easily complete) editing the shoot. Subsequent edits became easier and easier. Now the whole process, including slide retrieval, can be performed quickly.Here is how it works. After picking up a number of rolls of film from the lab, I immediately skim through each box, identifying the specific railroad and separating the slides (by road name) into labeled, empty, plastic slide boxes. All the Union Pacific go in one box, Santa Fe in another, and so on. Amtrak also goes into its own box even when the specific image was made on the UP or any other carrier's lines. I also use empty plastic slide boxes for non-railroad related slides, such as nature photos or pictures of friends. All the slide box labels have a one or two-word description (usually the location) along with the subject/road name. For example: Conrail/Selkirk or D&H/Tunkahannock. Sometimes I include the train

No written rule says every railroad image must feature the train or locomotive as the primary subject. Instead, look for a trackside element — either natural or man-made — and use it as the main subject, letting the train take a secondary role. It's even okay to allow the train to go out of focus or to blur if that makes a more creative photo.

(Opposite page) Just three more miles and southbound Kansas City Southern coal train No. 91 will be in Heavener, Oklahoma. After being refueled and recrewed, it will start the slow, arduous climb up Rich Mountain near the Arkansas border. Canon F-1, 300 mm, Fujichrome 100, 1/500th, f4

(Top) A Burlington Northern helper set — three SD40-2s and a fuel tender — pass by a solar panel used to power a defective equipment detector on Crawford Hill in the extreme north western part of Nebraska. Canon T90, 20 mm, Fujichrome 50, 1/125th, f6

(Bottom) A GP-10 and MT-4 slug make up trains at the west end of Conrail's Elkhart, Indiana, yard for an evening departure. Canon T90, 24 mm, Fujichrome 50, 1/60th, f11

123

symbol or name, such as Amtrak/California Zephyr or SP/Memphis Blue Streak. While categorizing at this stage, I also eliminate grossly over or under-exposed shots and blank slides.

After the preliminary review, I start a more closely honed edit. I look for "keepers" for a variety of uses, including book projects and/or railfan magazines. I might end up using six or seven labeled boxes marked: Book, Trains, Pacific Rail News, Passenger Train Journal, Nature, Miscellaneous, and so on. Of course, an infinite number of categories can be used. This depends on your own interests and needs. Other common groupings could include: Slides to Trade, Slides to Sell, Slide Show or Military Trains, Cabooses, Steam Engines, Bridges, and so on.

Think Quality Control

The first slides to see the bottom of the trash can during your edit should be the improperly exposed ones: those that are too dark or too light to hold acceptable color and detail. Next to go are those that are out of focus.

It's important to disconnect your emotions when editing your own photographs. All too often you may keep extremely poor slides because of fond memories of the day or trip. If it is really garbage, throw it out! Photos with uneven horizons, distracting features, and ineffective compositions should be weeded out and placed in an extra box marked "Outtakes."

If you are considering sending some of your images to a magazine, ensure that some variety exists from shot to shot and scene to scene. Editors don't want to edit for you, so avoid submitting redundant photos. Look closely at your slide sequences, and you'll find subtle differences that distinguish one shot from the next. It might be the reflection of a headlight glistening on the rails that sets one slide apart from the others. Another time, the unwanted shadow of a telephone pole across the lead locomotive or some background detail that went unnoticed when you were taking the photograph could ruin an otherwise beautiful shot. Two or three variations of a scene — perhaps one horizontal and two verticals (or vice versa) taken at varied distances — normally make a good sequence. The same editing method works well when you put together a tray or two of slides for family or friends. They'll enjoy your photography more if you use tighter quality control, and you'll most likely receive greater encouragement.

Preserving Your Images

The next concern after processing and editing your slides is their preservation. Several factors, either singularly or in concert, contribute to fading and deterioration: exposure to heat, humidity, light, gases, and vapors. All films, including Kodachrome, are vulnerable to long-term deterioration. You can't stop the ultimate destruction of your images. But fortunately, you can slow it down. Here's how to safeguard your slides for decades to come.

First, make sure your slide storage area is kept cool constantly, with the temperature rarely exceeding 70 degrees. Plus, avoid temperature extremes. Never keep your slides in an attic or cellar. Also, keep the humidity as low as possible to discourage fungus growth. An air conditioner helps quite a bit, but in really damp regions or homes, you may need to run a large capacity dehumidifier constantly.

Another contribution to fading is exposure to light, both ambient and during slide projection. Keep your slides in the dark for optimal archival storage. Holding projection time to a minimum when showing your favorite slides helps, too. (Both Ektachrome and Fujichrome film have greater resistance to projection fading than Kodachrome.)

Take great care when selecting slide pages, storage boxes, and cabinets for long-term safekeeping. Avoid polyvinyl chloride (PVC) slide pages at all costs. They eventually decompose and release harmful fumes that damage your slides. Instead, use the harmless polypropylene or polyethylene pages. If you prefer boxes to pages for slide storage, several different types of acid-free, archival-safe systems are available at reasonable prices. Wooden cabinets emit damaging vapors, so consider polypropylene storage boxes or baked enamel metal cabinets for large slide collections. Better camera stores carry many of these products, but Light Impressions of Rochester, New York, is the leading retail and mail-order company selling all types of archival supplies and books.

Copyrighting Your Photographs

Beyond physically protecting your photographs, you should also guard against their illegal use, especially if you plan to enter your work in contests or submit images to the train magazines. Copyright laws cover unpublished and published photos from the date that each picture was created and extend for the photographer's lifetime plus fifty years. The procedure for giving notice of copyright is easy and straightforward. Write by hand, use a rubber stamp, or affix a label directly on your slide mount or on the back print the following information: copyright, year, and photographer's name. (There is a copyright

Captivating railroad photographs needn't always include a train, locomotive, or even rolling stock. Here are three simple but attractive examples.

(Opposite page) A new day is dawning northeast of Tolono, Illinois, on Norfolk Southern's Detroit-St. Louis Line. Canon T90, 300 mm, Fujichrome 50, 1/500th, f5.6

(Next page) Sunset along the west shore of Lake Pend Oreille near Sand Point, Idaho. The former BN tracks now serve the Montana Rail Link. The fog in the scene was created artificially by breathing on the lens. Canon F-1, 85 mm, Fujichrome 100, 1/250th, f2.8

(Page 127) Ties and tracks, unknown location, unknown railroad.
Canon F-1, 200 mm, Fujichrome 100, 1/250th f6

symbol, ©, that you may prefer to use if you'd like to abbreviate. My copyright looks like this: © 1993 Gary J. Benson.)

There are several alternatives to writing or rubber stamping your copyright notice manually. The first, and least expensive, is to use adhesive-backed labels that can be run through your typewriter. Three more sophisticated variations of labeling, called Labelware, Labelbase, and Phototrak Superlabeler are used with your home computer and printer. As well as providing copyright notice, all are good ways to caption either individual groups of slides or entire collections. Light Impressions carries the software mentioned above.

If you shoot hundreds of rolls of film each year you might consider purchasing slide mounts imprinted with your copyright, address, and phone number. You can drop off your mounts and exposed film at a color lab, and pick up the processed and mounted slides. Pic-Mount is the only company I know that custom prints cardboard slide mounts. (Check with the labs in your area to see if they use cardboard mounts, and explain your desire to use your own mounts before ordering any.)

The last, most expensive, and most technological equipment for slide mount imprinting are the Trac Industries Slidetyper machines. These imprinters are the Rolls Royces of slide captioning equipment and are available in five models, ranging from $1,350 for the manual units to $4,500 for the top-of-the-line automatic version. Slidetypers are designed to be used with any computer, or Trac can supply an NEC/8300 entry system to input caption/copyright data. For example, the manual CM6 model, which sells for $1,550 including the NEC/8300, can imprint six lines of type on the wide portion of your slide mount — three on the top and three on the bottom — as well as four lines of type on the narrow portion — two on the top and two on the bottom. Railroad photographers with burgeoning slide collections or National Railroad Historical Society chapters with numerous active photographers as members could all benefit from these fine products.

Getting Your Photographs Published

One of the most exciting and rewarding aspects of photography is seeing one's work reproduced in print. Railroad photographers are fortunate to have a multitude of publications to approach with individual images or picture stories; they range from prototype railroad to model railroad magazines.

Getting published involves more than mere talent. You need to know what photos to submit and how, when, and to whom they should be submitted. It may seem obvious, but the first step is to study the magazines you are most interested in. Examine the types of photos they use most often. I'm not implying that you copy other photographer's photos or styles. But don't send freight shots to *Passenger Train Journal* or East Coast pictures to a West Coast magazine.

Next, look at the publication's masthead (which lists the staff by position) to find the name of the editorial assistant or managing editor. Write to that

person and ask them to mail you the magazine's guidelines for writers and photographers and the rates it pays for photography. The guidelines should answer your questions about the manner in which you should submit your images.

Since you now have the magazine's attention, you may want to outline briefly some of the photos you already have and mention upcoming projects you are considering. Because of the hectic schedules of most editorial staffs, allow a week or two for a response. Sending a self-addressed, stamped envelope with your request usually helps expedite matters. Should you not hear back after two weeks, call the magazine's contact person, and discuss your request over the phone.

The type of trains and railroads you photograph are dictated by your own interests and locale, while the requirements of each magazine are directed by the editorial content routinely covered. For comments by magazine editors regarding their photo needs see page 138. Although there are no guarantees, editing your train photos with the editor's needs in mind greatly increases your chances of being published.

How you package and send your photographs can even make a difference (in terms of making the magazine editor's job easier and in protecting your **127**

work from getting lost or damaged in transit). The following tips will help ensure that your best foot is put forward

• Make sure that each slide (or print) has a copyright notice and is captioned with all the pertinent information.

• Insert each slide into a clear polyester transview slide sleeve (available from Light Impressions) to guard against fingerprints and dust.

• Place the individual slides into clear polypropylene or polyethylene slide pages, twenty at a time.

• Make a delivery memo that dates and documents your submission: the number of photos

and description. Keep one copy for yourself, and send the original delivery memo to the magazine.

• Sandwich your slide pages (or prints), along with your delivery memo, between a few pieces of cardboard, and insert them into an envelope. Include a suitably sized self-addressed stamped envelope as well. Then, place all the material into a jiffy bag (for mailing or sending United Parcel Service) or a Federal Express pouch, if you are using a courier. Always use a traceable method when sending valuable photos.

Additionally, if you feel that your originals are extremely valuable, ship them overnight priority or have dupes made and send the dupes — stamped

Maintenance-of-way forces make good subjects because they work afield and are fairly accessible to photograph. I always ask the workers to wear their hard hats and goggles, if appropriate for the job they'll be doing in the photo. That way, no one gets in trouble if the photos get published.

(Far left) At the far east end of Conrail's Selkirk, New York, yard a butet welding crew repairs an old weld. In the background, the SENH (Selkirk to New Haven) waits for a clear signal to depart eastward. Canon EOS-1, 300 mm, Fujichrome Velvia 50, 1/250th, f5.6

(Above) In Elkhart, Indiana, a Conrail maintenance-of-way worker grinds down a fresh weld in Elkhart yard. Canon F-1, 35 mm, Fujichrome 100, 1/30th, f8

duplicate — by regular mail.

In many instances, magazines are looking for complete picture/text stories; so if you can write as well as take photos, you'll be better off. However, if you aren't as well versed in writing, you could ask around and team up with someone who is a good writer but not such a hot photographer.

Making multiple submissions of dissimilar photos to the various railroad publications further increases the likelihood of your pictures being printed. At all costs, avoid sending nearly identical images to several magazines simultaneously. The proper protocol is to approach one magazine at a time with a certain story or series of photos so as to avoid embarrassing duplicity.

Inevitably, all photographers, especially beginners, will have their pictures and story ideas rejected. Don't take it as a personal failure; consider it as part of the learning process. If it was easy to get published, it wouldn't be fun.

Other Markets

There are numerous additional options open to the train photographer who desires to be published: railroad books, calenders, ads, and, in some cases, even small railroad newsletters. Approach the publishers, manufacturers, and railroads in the same manner as you would the magazines. First, explain what you have and what you'd like to do. Ask them what they pay and then, if you're both interested, send them some photos (dupes whenever possible) and proceed from there.

Atmospheric conditions such as haze, fog, dust, and smoke alter the light illuminating your railroad subject and can become an integral part of the scene.

(Previous page) On a winter day in 1987, snow squalls cleared momentarily for a setting sun along Conrail's main line east of Erie, Pennsylvania. Canon F-1, 400 mm, Fujichrome 100, 1/500th, f4.5

(Left) On a rainy, foggy March 12, 1989, a pair of Soo Line 3,800-horsepower SD60s and a loaded coal train emerge from a fog bank on the Carrington Subdivision near Valley City, North Dakota. Canon F-1, 35 mm, Fujichrome 100, 1/125th, f3.5

(Right) Loram railgrinder No. 8 slowly works its way east on Southern Pacific's Del Rio Subdivision near Dryden, Texas, on March 22, 1991. Canon EOS-1, 80-200-mm zoom at 200 mm, Fujichrome 50, 1/250th, f5.6

Two of Conrail's 100-unit fleet of 4000-horsepower GE C40-8ws, adorned in the latest "Conrail Quality" paint scheme, guide GRA-43 along the banks of the Mohawk River near Fort Plain, New York. Originating in the midwest, the grain train will be at the Port of Albany for unloading in a matter of hours. Canon F-1, 35 mm lens, Fujichrome Velvia 50 pushed to ISO 100, 1/500th, f4.5

Getting your work published is often far from lucrative. Unfortunately, many, although certainly not all, individuals, agencies and publishers pay railfan photographers far less than a satisfactory rate for the use of their images. You'll need to weigh the low pay against the benefits of having a photograph published and decide for yourself.

Here are a few tips that you may find helpful when marketing your images:

• Read several books or magazine articles about selling your photography.

• Find out what the payment rate is prior to

sending any photos.

• Insist on a photo credit.

•Insist on payment plus a copy of the book/magazine/brochure in which your photos appear — not either/or.

• With larger magazines, insist that you are paid an absolute minimum of $35 per photo used (at least enough to cover the cost of a roll of film and processing, plus).

• Grant only one-time North American rights for the use of your photos, and put it in writing.

• Speak out loud and clear if you are dissatisfied with the payment offered.

• Realize that payment for the use of your photos in advertising and marketing should be significantly higher than for editorial use in books and magazines.

• When in doubt about what the accepted rate is for a specific photo usage, ask the opinion of a local commercial photographer.

Learning the ropes of getting your train photographs published is seldom as precarious as I've outlined here. However, a cautious outlook and approach will ensure enjoyable experiences for years to come.

An exquisite sunset marks the end of another day on Southern Pacific's Sunset route near Shawmut, Arizona. But the crew onboard 1AXDAT still has more than 100 miles to go before reaching Tucson, their crew change point. Canon F-1, 35 mm, Fujichrome 100, 1/500th, f3.5

Here is what the editors of four of the leading train magazines had to say about their photo needs.

• *Passenger Train Journal*, Carl Swanson, editor: "Each monthly issue of *Passenger Train Journal* features a wide range of photographs: everything from action scenes to three-quarter views of the latest passenger equipment. Since we cover just one segment of the railroad industry, our magazine probably receives fewer photo submissions than other national titles. Even so, we receive many more photos than we can use. But there are some things you can do to improve your chances of getting published.

"While first runs of passenger trains and major steam excursions usually trigger a flood of submissions, photos of Amtrak and commuter trains in daily operation are in relatively short supply at the magazine. Not only do we need these day-to-day shots to illustrate our news columns, we often need recent photos to accompany feature articles.

"Passenger trains, with their colorfully painted equipment, sleek consists, and predictable schedules, have a lot to offer the railroad photographer. In general, if it's happening in North American passenger railroading, we want to see your photos of it."

• *Trains*, Dave Ingles, Senior Editor: "We generally look for photographs to fulfill three functions in the magazine. First, we depend on a steady influx of news-oriented pictures for our monthly section called Railroad News Photos. In this category, the accent isn't so much on quality but on news value and timeliness, although we strive for as much quality as possible.

"Second, as we have done for fifty years, we continue to build our files of feature photographs, which help us fill our Photo Section, illustrate feature articles, or serve as photo essays on specific subjects. Although our decisions are admittedly subjective, we generally save only what we consider to be the best photos. These are analyzed from both compositional (or artistic) merits, as well as technical standpoints.

"Finally, we are devoting more time to developing cover photographs, which have the dual purposes of enhancing editorial product and serving as a point-of-purchase marketing tool. Because virtually all our covers relate directly to a story in each issue, this is a sometimes difficult procedure; but we are doing more advance legwork to ensure we have the ideal cover shot."

• *Pacific Rail News*, Don Gulbrandsen, Editor: "At *Pacific Rail News* we are looking for quality action photography of western and midwestern rail subjects. Technical quality is of primary importance, as is composition. Subject matter (i.e., how newsworthy a

photo is) can influence our photo editing, but we tend to get a lot of photos of the biggest news events and from the most popular locales. Thus, it all comes back to which photo is in focus, well exposed, and best composed when we pick one.

"Three factors enhance how we view a railroad photograph: the backdrop, location, and dynamism. Unfortunately, we get an overabundance of train-only wedge shots. Railroads are part of the American landscape; and by including part of the landscape — trackside structures, farms, trees, even people — in a train photo, you give the whole image more impact, and you have a better chance of getting published. Relatedly, we get too many shots of the same old locations — Cajon, Tehachapi, Sherman Hill, and so on. What really catches our eyes is a shot from a little-known line — a picture that can also tell a story that readers aren't familiar with. Finally, railroads are a dynamic subject. We like photos that convey movement, power, even battle of man versus nature. They have a better chance of getting published than a standard roster shot.

"Black and white or color? We run roughly half color and half black and white, and we pay a premium for black-and-white prints to encourage their submission. But, because so many people shoot strictly slides, we have found it essential to be adaptable. Thus, we've found an outstanding and inexpensive system for converting slides to black and white; we clearly get the best results among rail magazines. The upshot: We're flexible and can reproduce with quality anything but snapshot-size color prints and high-speed slide film (K200 is the fastest we'll tolerate). And, two key rules for submission: Put your name and address on every photo; and include detailed caption information. You can't tell us too much."

•*Railfan & Railroad*, Jim Boyd, Editor: "Our photo needs are predominantly news oriented. Just sending us your neatest pictures doesn't help us out unless they are newsworthy or relate to a feature article. We need both black and white and color; so if you shoot both, send both.

"From the standpoint of submitting other material to us, you are generally much better off writing a story and sending photos than merely sending individual shots. Keep in mind that we aren't a photography magazine, we are a railroad magazine. We need news photos that could, perhaps, stand alone without a caption. Well-lighted roster shots are fine if the subject is the locomotive itself (an unusual or new model or paint scheme); but if the story is about a location or newsworthy operation, try to show the train in context. If the story is about a Santa Fe unit showing up on Conrail, the photo should put the unit in a distinctly Conrail setting. This also applies to feature material. If you're shooting a shortline that serves a paper mill, don't get all wound up and only photograph their Alcos out in the snow, crossing bridges, and running through the countryside. I want to see photographs of the train and its consist — the wood chip gondolas or log cars — at the smoky, gritty paper mill. That's why the train exists!

"For news photos, I don't want anything funky or artsy-craftsy. For feature photos, I need a variety of shots — different angles, verticals, horizontals, twilight shots, sunset shots, and nighttime shots. Night photos are great because they add a very distinct visual variety to a set of images. Additionally, I'm looking for one or two real 'screamers' for lead photos and potential covers. But bear in mind that cover shots are not just horizontal compositions made with the camera turned on end.

"Color submissions should be chromes as they are much easier for us to work with. Larger formats are okay to send, but unfortunately too many people tend to send us 'garbage' shots on 2 1/4" and 4"x5" transparencies that would be rejects in 35 mm. Just because the film size is bigger doesn't make it a better photo. As far as shooting color neg, it's got to be a really good color print, on hard glossy paper, to equal the quality of chrome film. Glossy 5"x7" and 8"x10" black-and-white shots should have a nice representation of highlights, mid-tones, and shadow detail."

Silhouetted against the western sky, a quartet of tank cars trails a trio of eastbound Southern Pacific locomotives near Fenner, Arizona, on Espee's Lordsburg Subdivision. Canon T90, 20 mm, Fujichrome 50, 1/500th, f6.7

On a stormy Sunday morning in November 1990, a duo of Amtrak AEM7s race across the Susquehanna River at Havre de Grace, Maryland, with a long train of coaches and baggage cars in tow. Canon T90, 20 mm, Fujichrome Velvia 50, 1/8th, f4

Closing remarks

With safety being your first priority, be as aggressive as you can in your photographic endeavors. If necessary, borrow or rent a boat to get an unusual view of a commonplace rail scene. Try shooting up at trains when everybody else is shooting down. Use a telephoto lens when your buddies insist that a normal or wide angle is the only answer. Experiment with slow shutter speeds that may transform a routine photo into an extraordinary image. Climb that cliff you've always thought about shooting from and make, perhaps, a photo that's never been made before. Work at making each of your train shots special. Learn to be selective about the tools and techniques you use, as well as the weather conditions and locations in which you work. What you get out of railroad photography is directly related to the time and effort you put into it. Lastly, in your quest for great images, don't lose sight of the primary goal of railroad photography — just having fun.

References

The following names, addresses, and phone numbers of the manufacturers, producers, publishers, and services mentioned in this book may be helpful to you if you would like further information about their products or services. Many companies will gladly send you a brochure, technical data sheet, or catalog free of charge.

Film

Agfa Corporation
100 Challenger Rd.
Ridgefield Park, NJ 07644
(201) 440-2500

Eastman Kodak Company
343 State St.
Rochester, NY 14650
(716) 724-4447

Fuji Photo
555 Taxter Rd.
Elmsford, NY 10523
(914) 789-8100
1-800- 659-3854
1-800-326-0800

Film Processing

Duggal Color Projects
9 West 20th St.
New York, NY 10011
(212) 242-7000

Maps

County Maps
Puetz Place
Lydon Station, WI 53944
(608) 666-3331

DeLorme Mapping
P.O. Box 298
Freeport, ME 04032
1-800-227-1656

United States Geological Survey-ESIC
507 National Center
Reston, VA 22092
1-800-USA-MAPS

Photography Books

A Photographer's Place
133 Mercer St.

New York, NY 10012
(212) 431-9358

Amphoto
1515 Broadway
New York, NY 10036
(212) 536-5101

Gould Trading
7 East 17th St.
New York, NY 10003
(212) 243-2306
1-800-367-4854
(Extensive selection of photo books, photo equipment)

The Saunders Group
21 Jet View Drive
Rochester, NY 14624
(716) 328-7800
(Sells *Hove Camera Manuals* for Canon, Nikon, Minolta and Pentax users. They are comprehensive guides that feature in-depth information about the functions and operation of current model cameras.)

Visual Departures
1641 3rd Ave, Suite 202
New York, NY 10128
(212) 534-1718
1-800-628-2003
(Source for Jon Falk's Adventures in Location Lighting)

Photography Equipment -Manufacturers/Distributors

Balcar Tekno
100 W. Erie St.
Chicago, IL 60610
(312) 787-8922
(Balcar Monolights — high-powered electronic flash equipment)

Bogen Photo Corporation
565 East Crescent Ave,
P.O. Box 506

Ramsey, NJ 07446-0506
(Tripods and mid-powered portable Metz electronic flash units)

Broncolor/Sinar Bron
17 Progress St.
Edison, NJ 08820
(908) 754-5800
(Impact Monolights — high-powered electronic flash)

Bronica
GMI Photographic Inc.
1776 New Highway,
P.O. Drawer U
Farmingdale, NY 11735
(516) 752-0066
(Medium format cameras and lenses)

Canon USA
One Canon Plaza
Lake Success, NY 11042
(516) 488-6700
(Cameras and lenses)

Comet
311-319 Long Ave.
Hillside, NJ 07205-2089
(908) 688-3210
(High-powered electronic flash equipment)

Dyna-Lite
311-319 Long Ave.
Hillside, NJ 07205
(908) 687-8800
(High-powered electronic flash equipment)

EG & G Electro-Optics
35 Congress St.
Salem, MA 01970
(508) 745-3200
(Photo Flash Bulbs)

Fuji Photo
555 Taxter Rd.
Elmsford, NY 10523
(914) 789-8100
(Medium format cameras)

Leica Camera, Inc.
156 Ludlow Ave.
Northvale, NJ 07647

(201) 767-7500
(Billingham Camera Bags)

Lowe Pro USA
2194 Northpoint Parkway
Santa Rosa, CA 95407
(Camera Bags)

Lumedyne
6010 Wall St.
Port Richey, FL 34668
(813) 847-5394
(High-powered portable electronic
flash equipment)

Mamiya America Corporation
8 Westchester Plaza
Elmsford, NY 10523
(914) 347-3300
(Medium Format Cameras)

Minolta Corporation
101 Williams Drive
Ramsey, NJ 07446
(201) 825-4000
(Cameras, lenses and auxilliary
light meters)

Nikon Inc.
1300 Walt Whitman Rd.
Melville, NY 11747
(516) 222-0200
(Cameras and lenses)

Norman Enterprises, Inc.
P.O. Box 7749
Burbank, CA 91510
(213) 843-6811
(Portable electronic flash
equipment)

Olympus
145 Crossways Park Drive
Woodbury, NY 11797
(516) 364-3000
(Cameras and lenses)

Pentax
35 Inverness Drive East
Englewood, CO 80155
(303) 799-8000
(35-mm and medium format
cameras)

Quantum Instruments
1075 Stewart Ave.
Garden City, NY 11530

(516) 222-0611
(Strobe Batteries/Radio Remotes)

Satter, Inc.
4100 Dahlia St.
Denver, CO 80216
(303) 399-7493
(Camera bags, Sea King cases)

Saunders
21 Jet View Drive
Rochester, NY 14624
(716) 328-5602
(Domke camera bags/Benbo
tripods)

Schneider Corporation of America
400 Crossways Park Drive
Woodbury, NY 11797
(516) 496-8500
(B&W brand filters for color and
black and white)

Speedotron
310 South Racine Ave.
Chicago, IL 60607
(312) 421-4050
(High powered electronic flash
equipment)

Tamrac
9240 Jordan Ave
Chatsworth, CA 91311
1-800-662-0717
(Camera bags, photo vests)

Tocad
10 Hackensack Ave.
Hackensack, NJ 07601
(201) 342-2400
(Sunpack portable electronic
flash equipment)

Uniphot Corporation
61-10 34th Ave.
Woodside, NY 11377
(718) 779-5700
(Tiltall tripods)

Photography Equipment — Repair

Nippon Photo Clinic
920 Broadway, 7th Floor
New York, NY 10010
(212) 673-7530

Strauss Technical Photo Service
1240 Mount Olivet Rd. N.E.
Washington, DC 20002
(202) 529-3200

Photography Equipment — Retail Sales/Rentals

Calumet Photographic
890 Supreme Drive
Bensenville, IL 60106
1-800-225-8638

Ken Hansen Photographic
920 Broadway, 5th Floor
New York, NY 10010
(212) 777-5900

PhoTak
P.O. Box 2104
Neenah, WI 54957
(414) 722-8733
(Great camera and lighting gear
and finger mittens. Also, publishes
an informative newsletter)

Photography Magazines

Outdoor Photograper
Werner Publishing Corporation
16000 Ventura Blvd, Suite 800
Encino, CA 91436
(818) 986-8400

Photo District News
49 East 21st St.
New York, NY 10010
(212) 677-8418
Shutterbug
Patch Publishing
5211 S. Washington Ave.
Titusville, FL 32780
(407) 268-5010

Photography Workshops

Palm Beach Photographic
Workshops
600 Fairway Drive, Suite 104
Deerfield Beach, FL 33441
1-800-553-2622; (407) 391-7557

The Maine Photographic
Workshops
Rockport, ME 04856
(207) 236-8581

RIT Photo Workshop Series
One Lomb Memorial Drive
Rochester, NY 14623
(716) 475-2200

Santa Fe Photographic
Workshops

P.O. Box 9916
Santa Fe, NM 85704
1-800-388-3258

Serbin Communications
511 Olive St.
Santa Barbara, CA 93101
(805) 963-0439
Publisher of Photography &
Travel Workshop Directory
(A comprehensive directory of
workshops offered throughout the
U.S. and abroad)

Railroad Books

DPA-LTA Enterprise Inc.
P.O. Box 728
Rouses Point, NY 12979-0728
1993 Official Locomotive Rosters

John Szwajkart
P.O. Box 163
Brookfield, IL 60513
Train Watcher's Guides —
Chicago, Kansas City and St. Louis

Kalmbach Books
21027 Crossroads Circle
P.O. Box 1612
Waukesha, WI 53187
1-800-533-6644
(Railroad reference series: *The
American Shortline Railway
Guide - 4th edition*; *Compendium
of American Railroad Radio
Frequencies - 12th edition*; *The
Contemporary Diesel Spotter's
Guide*; *Diesel Locomotive Rosters,
U.S., Canada, Mexico - 3rd
edition*; *Historical Guide to North
American Railroads*; *The Train
Watcher's Guide to North
American Railroads - 2nd edition*)

Old Line Graphics
1604 Woodwell Rd.
Silver Spring, MD 20906
(301) 460-9193
The *Railroad Night Scene* and
other titles.

Railroad Magazines

Extra 2200 South
Box 8110-820
Blaine, WA 98230-2107

Passenger Train Journal
Pacific Rail News
Interurban Press
P.O. Box 6128
Glendale, CA 91225
(818) 240-9130

Railfan & Railroad Magazine
Carstens Publications Inc.
Phil Hardin Rd, P.O. Box 700
Fredon Township
Newton, NJ 07860-0700

Railpace News Magazine
P.O. Box 927
Piscataway, NJ 08855-0927

Trains
Kalmbach Publishing
21027 Crossroads Circle, P.O.
Box 1612
Waukesha, WI 53187
(414) 796-8776; 1-800-446-5489

Railroad Timetables

Carl Loucks
464 Washington Ave.
North Haven, CT 06473

Railroad Videos

Green Frog Productions
200 N. Cobb Parkway, Building
100/Suite 138
Marietta, GA 30062
1-800-227-1336; (404) 442-2220

Greg Scholl Video Productions
P.O. Box 123
Batavia, Ohio 45103
(513) 732-0660

Hopewell Productions
1714 Boardman-Poland Rd. #15.
Poland, OH 44514
1-800-722-0765

Pentrex
P.O. Box 94911
Pasadena, CA 91109
1-800-950-9333

Railroad Video Productions
281 Willow Dell Lane
Leola, PA 17540
1-800-258-4546
(717) 656-8733

Video Rails
P.O. Box 80001
San Diego, CA 92138
1-800-262-2776

WB Video Productions
6447 S. Heritage Place W.
Englewood, CO 80111
1-800-448-3987; (303) 770-8421

Scanners

Cobra Electronics
6500 West Cortland St.
Chicago, IL 60635
(312) 889-4905

Scanner World USA
10 New Scotland Ave.
Albany, NY 12208
(518) 436-9606

Uniden Bearcat
9900 West Point Drive
Indianapolis, IN 46250
(317) 842-2483

Slide Editing Equipment and Supplies

Light Impressions
439 Monroe Ave.
Rochester, NY 14607-3717
1-800-828-6216
(Archival supplies, light tables,
etc.)

Pic-Mount
2300 Arrow Head Drive
Carson City, NV 89706
(702) 887-5100
(Slide mounts, slide boxes)

Trac Industries
26 Old Limekiln Rd.
Doylestown, PA 18901
(215) 345-9311
(Slide captioning imprinters)

Index

A Norfolk and Southern diamond, polished to a mirror-like finish by each passing freight, glistens in the sun at Fort Wayne, Indiana. Canon T90, 14-mm, Fujichrome 50, 1/125th, f8.5

RAILROAD LOG

Train # / Symbol _____ Loads _____   Empties _____ Tons _____

Day _____ Date _____   TIme AM _____ PM _____

Div _____   Sub Div _____

Road_____ MP_____   Direction _____

Location _____   Nearest City _____

   Lead Loco / Road / Make   Other Units / Road / Make

#_____ / _____ /_____   #_____ / _____ /_____

Consist _____   #_____ / _____ /_____

Weather Conditions _____   #_____ / _____ /_____

_____   #_____ / _____ /_____

Equipment / Lenses Used   #_____ / _____ /_____

Camera _____ Lens _____   Film_____

Shutter_____   F-Stop _____

Other Remarks _____

_____

_____

_____